Educational Leadership and Management
Developing insights and skills

Marianne Coleman and Derek Glover

Open University Press

Open University Press
McGraw-Hill Education
McGraw-Hill House
Shoppenhangers Road
Maidenhead
Berkshire
England
SL6 2QL

email: enquiries@openup.co.uk
world wide web: www.openup.co.uk

and Two Penn Plaza, New York, NY 10121-2289, USA

First published 2010

A catalogue record of this book is available from the British Library

ISBN-13: 978-0-33-523608-4 (pb) 978-0-33-523609-1 (hb)
ISBN-10: 0-33-523608-1 (pb) 0-33-523609-X (hb)

Library of Congress Cataloging-in-Publication Data
CIP data applied for

Typeset by Aptara Inc., India
Printed in the UK by Bell and Bain Ltd, Glasgow.

Fictitous names of companies, products, people, characters and/or data that
may be used herein (in case studies or in examples) are not intended to
represent any real individual, company, product or event.

Mixed Sources
Product group from well-managed
forests and other controlled sources
www.fsc.org   Cert no. TT-COC-002769
© 1996 Forest Stewardship Council

FSC

The McGraw·Hill Companies

Contents

Introduction

The focus of this book is the range of interpersonal skills associated with leadership and management in education. We are addressing the range of skills needed by leaders and managers and aim to provide them with fresh insights on how they carry out their daily work in the dynamic world of education.

The origins and ethos of the book

The origins of this book lie in a module that is part of an MA in educational management and leadership taught at the Institute of Education, University of London. The module was originally developed by Anne Gold for face to face teaching, and Anne has kindly written an important chapter in this book on values in educational leadership. The face to face module was then developed for use in distance learning by Marianne Coleman and Derek Glover in an MA in applied educational leadership and management offered by the External Programme of the University of London and taught through the Institute of Education. Megan Crawford, who has contributed a chapter drawing on her recent research on leadership and emotion, has taught both the face to face and distance learning modules. As the main authors, Marianne and Derek value the experience and specialist knowledge that Anne and Megan have brought to the book.

The book has developed well beyond its origins in the face to face or distance learning iterations of the course. It also differs from other books in the area of educational leadership and management as it is firmly placed in the context of diversity and equity. The book has been written to include the particular insights and skills that leaders in education need to successfully lead and manage people within a culturally diverse and inclusive society.

This book is intended for interested practitioners and for students of educational leadership and management who might be studying for Masters, taught doctoral programmes or professional courses and who have an interest in the promotion of social justice.

Special features

The special features of the book include the following:

- The book aims to bring together theory and practice on aspects of educational leadership and management.
- All the chapters include an illustrative scenario drawn from real life situations.
- It encourages a reflective approach.
- Leadership is generally understood to be distributed rather than vested in one leader.
- It promotes an ethical stance based on values of social justice and equity.
- There is a focus on cultural diversity.
- The authors are able to draw on their own research.

Theory and practice

The first aim of the authors is to bring together theory and practice in the context of leading and managing adults who work in education. Each chapter focuses on an aspect of leading and managing and goes beyond lists of 'how to', to examine some of the deeper theoretical issues that relate to, for example, motivation, decision-making, communication and difference.

Scenarios

The practical aspects of leading and managing are explored in every chapter through a scenario drawn from real life illustrating relevant leadership and management challenges. Through the scenarios you are invited to examine your own values and understanding of your work in education and to actively engage with theories and concepts that underpin the practical aspects of leadership and management in education. We acknowledge our debt to our students and practitioners who have provided us with material on which to base the scenarios. All of them are based on real situations, and also draw on the authors' experiences as teachers, researchers, consultants and governors. Details and names have been changed to protect the anonymity of students and institutions.

Reflection

In every chapter, readers are invited to reflect on their own practice in light of the discussions. As leaders they are also encouraged to reflect on the practice, taking time to consider the impact and consequences of their actions and to practise empathy and emotional intelligence (Chapter 10 is devoted to the interplay of emotions and leadership).

Leadership

Leadership is a huge area and this book is concerned mainly with aspects of people management rather than, for example, strategic or financial leadership. In practice, we tend to blur the distinction between leadership and management, as it is often the same people who are undertaking both. The authors see leadership as particularly associated with setting the values and the vision of an organization or group, and management as the more day to day enactment of the vision.

The authors also recognize that educational institutions normally have a titular leader – it could be a principal, a head teacher, a vice chancellor – but that it is now accepted that leadership can be distributed among a range of people within the institution. The distribution of leadership recognizes that teachers and lecturers, who are professionals in education, may exercise their own powers of leadership in the classroom, or in a tutorial situation. They may also lead a team or a department or have other cross-institutional responsibilities for example relating to the development of information and communication technology (ICT) or for pastoral work.

The ways in which leadership is exercised by individuals will depend on the prevailing culture and leadership style which normally emanates from the senior leader(s). You are likely to have some knowledge of the range of leadership styles, but for an authoritative review see Bush (2003). The extent to which leadership is successfully distributed will depend on the development of a clear and inspiring vision and values for the organization and the communication of the vision and values.

Social justice and equity

There is current interest in the importance of moral leadership and of values in leadership (see for example the National College for Leadership of Schools and Children's Services website: www.nationalcollege.org.uk). This book holds values in leadership and management as central to practice. The values upheld in the book are within a stance of social justice and democracy and the promotion of equal opportunities and inclusivity and the valuing of diversity. Chapters 1 and 2 focus on these areas.

Cultural diversity

An important feature of the book also arises from social justice and it is a focus on cultural diversity. Schools and colleges in the UK and throughout the world are increasingly peopled by students and staff who come from diverse ethnic, cultural and religious backgrounds. Most of the books concerned with educational leadership and management tend to presume a homogeneous staff and student body and those written in the UK are generally anglo-centric in their approach. This book is written by UK authors who have wide experience of working internationally, who are able to present leadership and management insights from international sources and a range of cultures. The book is therefore appropriate for educationalists of the twenty-first century operating within the confines of a particular country, in this case the UK, but actually inhabiting a global environment. However, the authors recognize that the book is rooted in Western concepts of democracy.

As you read this book it will be useful to bear in mind a particularly helpful theory developed by Gert Hofstede (1991), who identified five dimensions relating to cultural differences between nations. These are:

- *Individualism–collectivism:* the degree to which people value the individual or the group. In Western cultures like the USA and the UK the individual and individualism is greatly valued. In China, for example, there has traditionally been greater value placed on the group or the family than the individual.
- *Power distance:* the social and emotional distance between leaders and led. Again in the USA and other Western countries there is relatively little power distance between an employer and an employee, and greater distance in more formal societies.
- *Uncertainty avoidance:* this dimension relates to the extent that people feel threatened by unknown or uncertain situations.
- *Masculinity–femininity:* this dimension refers to the stereotypical idea of masculine values of achievement and feminine values which are more people oriented, valuing good relationships.
- *Long-term versus short-term orientation.*

It is possible to 'map' the position of countries on the Hofstede dimensions. However, it is also worth remembering that positions do not remain static; social and technological change take place with increasing contact between workers in different countries. For example Chen et al. (2005) expected that Chinese subjects who they studied working in the field of technology would avoid conflict (in line with uncertainty avoidance and loss of face) but this was no longer the case as: 'the top management teams . . . confronted so many conflicts in the high technology environment of the rapidly developing Chinese marketplace that avoiding conflict was clearly understood to be unrealistic' (Chen et al. 2005: 292).

Drawing on original research

Throughout the book you will find references to the research that the authors have undertaken and which they draw on to illustrate aspects of their chapters. All authors have researched widely, but the areas that they draw on in the book mainly relate to diversity including ethnicity (Derek and Marianne), gender (Marianne), values in leadership (Anne) and emotions and leadership (Megan).

The content of the book

Leaders in education are faced by a rapidly changing context and do not always have time to reflect on what the changes actually mean, and how to operationalize them. The authors hope that this book will help them reflect on their practice as they lead and manage the staff in their schools and colleges.

Chapter 1 focuses on the conceptual nature of diversity and, through a real example of a head teacher's dilemma, brings out some of the difficult issues that relate to leading and managing the staff and other stakeholders in a modern urban school. Leading with values is a core theme of the book and Chapter 2 by Anne Gold focuses on this area. Chapters 1 and 2 both emphasize the need to take time to reflect on what you consider important in leadership.

Chapter 3 takes the issue of values and leadership to consider how best these are communicated in an educational institution, focusing then on the ways in which communications can be effective in groups and between individuals. Chapter 4 looks at a vital aspect of leadership and management, that of decision-taking and then considers how best to go about the management of conflict where decisions are disputed.

Chapters 5 and 6 look at the related areas of motivation, delegation and performance management, while Chapter 7 is concerned with working in and with teams and Chapter 8 the related area of leading and managing the meetings that tend to play such an important part in teamworking.

Chapter 9 focuses on the importance to individuals and their organizations of both time management and the management of stress, while Chapter 10 considers the still new and exciting juxtaposition of emotions with leadership. Chapter 11 brings the book to a close by focusing on how adults and their communities learn for the development of both individuals and their institutions.

It is unlikely that a book of this type will be read from start to finish, but you will find that there are many links between the chapters and every effort has been made to ensure that the reader is aware of the links.

We hope that the book proves to be of practical use and that it provides you with fresh insights into leading and managing within the dynamic world of education.

1 Leading and managing for diversity and social justice

Social justice and the valuing of diversity are the principles that underpin our approach to leadership in this book and we hope that this approach will provide you with new and valuable insights into educational leadership and management. This chapter specifically focuses on diversity and social justice, clarifying what we mean by those terms. Through the presentation and discussion of a true incident we then explore some of the implications for leaders in education.

What do we mean by diversity?

In general speech 'diversity' means 'many and different', but when currently used in relation to people, it is a word that has political overtones and is continually undergoing subtle changes in meaning. It is increasingly equated with ethnicity, but can also have a wider definition (as it does in this book), encompassing gender, disability, religion and age: areas that are now subject to laws relating to equal opportunities in the UK. Some of these differences are obvious and affect our perceptions of people, for example gender and age. Other differences are less obvious; for example class, or even differing personality types. The work of Belbin (1993) (see Chapter 6) focuses on this latter type of diversity and indicates that teams work better when they include a range of different personality types who complement each other. Diversity can therefore celebrate difference, but the other side of the coin is where somebody who is 'different' is judged against the majority or against an 'in-group' and their difference is somehow perceived as problematic.

The 'differences' between people that are implicit in the word diversity can and do cause conscious and unconscious hostility between individuals and groups and the differences are numerous: 'Diversity, in its broadest sense, has been defined as anything people could use to tell themselves that another person is different' (Jehn et al. 2008: 128). As people perceive others, they tend to categorize them and make use of stereotypes in doing so. This categorization occurs more easily with obvious physical and visible manifestations of difference, for example, skin colour or some types of physical disability, whereas stereotypes relating to non-visible differences such as class often arise from our understanding of power relations, for example employment status. Stereotyping saves us time in allowing quick judgements, and generally works to preserve the status quo (Fiske and Lee 2008). This is not to the advantage of newcomers, who are then likely to be regarded with hostility as 'outsiders'. People hold onto and justify their stereotypes and tend to have selective recall that supports their beliefs. There is a tendency to relate most easily to those we identify as most like ourselves. It has been known for some time that the 'gatekeepers' who make up selection panels have a tendency to appoint people in their own image (Morgan et al. 1983). This discrimination may be unthinking and simply reflect the internalized categorization of groups:

> Outgroups do not necessarily have to be hated to be targets of discrimination in hiring and promotion: more often, they are consistently passed over for others in the in-group, so they are in fact, excluded.
>
> (Fiske and Lee 2008: 21)

Social justice

The ideal of social justice provides an impetus to overcome discriminatory behaviour towards 'outsiders'. It recognizes that people are not treated equally, and implies intervention to change institutions and society towards being more just. Social justice is an overarching ideal, but it can inform the ways in which individuals, groups and institutions operate at all levels. Social justice is a liberal stance, placing value on each individual with a sense of: 'insistence on the separateness of one life from another, and the equal importance of each life, seen on its own terms rather than as part of a larger organic or corporate whole' (Nussbaum 1999: 10).

The business case for diversity

Social justice forms the main case for valuing diversity, but the second basis is the so-called 'business case'. This is the recognition that economic and other decisions might be better if we are 'making maximum use of the talent available in the labour pool' (Kulik and Roberson 2008: 265) rather than exclusively by those who are most likely to be in powerful positions; generally in Western societies, white, middle- and upper-class males (Equality and Human Rights Commission 2008). There is increasing recognition that a broader base for decision-making makes good economic sense. For example, including women in boards of directors, most of which have been all male, seems sensible, particularly as most consumer decisions are made by women. Research in the USA has shown that having three rather than the token one or two women on a corporate board improves the quality of decision-making and ultimately profit levels (Kramer et al. 2006) although there are contradictory findings relating to the link between diversity and work output (Jackson et al. 2003). However, there is a strong moral and practical argument that:

> Civil society depends on an appreciation of diversity – especially within the modern world of global communication, travel and trade. Successful societies can no longer sustain themselves if they are based on homogenous communities and are at war with those who are different from themselves.
>
> (North West Change Centre of Manchester Business School 2002: 1)

Diversity in education

The social justice and business case for diversity both apply in education, if we are to fully prepare young people for the globalization of the twenty-first century. As educators it is important to be aware of different viewpoints and to be free from the constraints that a single viewpoint brings. We need a more incisive and uncluttered view of society:

> Although we know that one pair of glasses does not fit all, as a culture, we are expected to use a common lens to view our world. This lens is a lens ground in the framework of the dominant culture. As a result we come to know our world through images that reflect the deeply embedded values and beliefs derived from a dominant culture of white, middle-class heterosexual males. Other perspectives which do not reflect the norms and standards of this dominant culture become blurred or rendered invisible.
>
> (Gosetti and Rusch 1995: 14)

Reflection

Looking at society through a lens that is not that of the dominant culture can be both exciting and instructive.

The introduction to this chapter has briefly reviewed the concepts of diversity and social justice, considering the 'natural' tendency to brand people who are different from the norm as 'outsiders' and then reviewing the social justice and business arguments for increasing diversity. This implies overcoming the natural tendency to label and stereotype which can lead the way to prejudice and discrimination.

The following example is an account of a true incident in an urban school in the UK with an ethnically diverse student intake.

Scenario: Racism in an English school – the head's story

One of the most difficult situations that I had to deal with in my first year of headship was responding to an incident which occurred outside of school but which was very much connected to events that had happened during the school day. For me it highlighted how the values of the head teacher, in terms of social justice and equity, must be translated into the practice of leadership and decision-making.

The individual students concerned

James is a white boy of middle-class parents. They had reluctantly sent James to the local school at his request. At the time of the incident James was a very happy and settled student who enjoyed school, attended well and made a positive contribution.

Dwayne is a 'looked after' child of dual heritage with a very troubled past and was on the verge of permanent exclusion from his primary school. At the time of the incident, he had settled very well at secondary school and was thriving from the support he was being given. He had received no other exclusions during the year.

Aaron, Jamahl and Leon are pupils of black Caribbean heritage.

What occurred

During the spring term a year 7 boy (Dwayne) had an altercation with a boy from year 8 (James) at lunchtime during which threats were made about following this up on the way home. It was unclear as to who had instigated the conflict and James did not think at the time that the threats were anything more than bravado. None of this was reported to a member of staff.

On the way home James, who was walking with two friends, became aware that he was being followed by a group of students from a range of years and led by Dwayne. About half a mile from school Dwayne rushed at James and kicked him; he encouraged three of his friends Aaron, Jamahl and Leon, who were also in year 7, to join in and they punched him. A large group of students (around 30) had gathered to watch. The assault was stopped when a member of the public pulled up in their car and got out to help James. At this point the crowd dispersed and James was taken home by the car driver. His parents took James to hospital for examination but he did not need any treatment.

The follow-up

On being informed of this incident the following morning, the school set about the usual investigations. The police had also been informed by James' parents and were conducting their own investigation. I took a decision fairly quickly to exclude all four boys for varying lengths of time. This was based on my knowledge of the students and my perception that the boys were all part of a friendship group and the involvement of Aaron, Jamahl and Leon was spontaneous rather than premeditated. In addition to the exclusions, I wrote to the parents of all the students who had been identified as part of the 'crowd' and spoke to all students in assemblies to appeal for further information. I decided not to permanently exclude Dwayne but to go for a fixed-term exclusion which involved the governing body and a plan for reintegration. I suggested a compromise of a fresh start at another school but, rightly, Dwayne's social worker would not support this. Dwayne was out of school for 60 days in total.

The aftermath

From the outset, James' parents began a campaign to brand the incident as a racist attack by a black gang. They tried to mobilize a group of parents from the feeder primary school that their son had attended, encouraging them to boycott the school. They threatened press involvement, contacted their local Member of Parliament (MP), councillors and the local authority. I maintained my stance and my rationale, stating that as head teacher I reserved the right to make decisions that were in the best interests of all parties, not just their son. I was certain that I had behaved justly and that the sanctions applied were appropriate. Dwayne's social worker was in support of the decision and wanted Dwayne to remain at the school where he had been making good progress until this incident. James returned to school for a time but was then withdrawn by his parents, against his wishes. I had several heated telephone conversations and exchanged letters with James' parents, particularly his mother, who would not accept my decision and continued to lobby for it to be overturned. I too contacted the local authority for advice. James' parents were also pressuring the police to take serious action and succeeding in persuading them to charge Dwayne for racially aggravated assault.

Turning points

The campaign reached a peak when, on the night of the school's open evening for parents of prospective year 7 students, James' parents leafleted those attending with a piece of propaganda describing the black students in the school as a gang who prowled the site looking for victims. By this time, James had returned to school, although Dwayne was still excluded. On the open evening James was in school helping staff as his parents were campaigning on his behalf at the school gates. I asked his mother how she could reconcile her lack of support for the school with James' contribution to the school; she could not offer a response. I was so incensed that I felt it necessary to take action, first, by explaining in my address to the prospective parents what the leaflet referred to, and second, by challenging the overt racism expressed by James' parents. As a black head teacher I found the leaflet's description of black students personally offensive. I was incensed by the fact that a friendship group was being called a gang and the students likened to animals. In response, I wrote a strong letter to James' parents to the effect that the local authority legal team would be looking into the situation and expressing my view that they were inciting racial tension in a school with a strong record of racial harmony. The leadership team and the governing body were in full support of my actions.

A further incident highlighted James' parents' beliefs. James had been hit accidentally during a physical education lesson; his father came to collect him from school and the first thing he said to James was 'Is it those niggers again?'. This was reported to me immediately by my colleagues. Again I wrote to the parents with further ammunition to support my perceptions about their racism. I received an apology for the use of the racist language and as it became clear that I was not going to change my stance, they realized they had been exposed and we needed to find a way forward. The police by this time had made a prosecution; Dwayne had pleaded guilty to assault. The additional charge of racially aggravated assault was dismissed.

Resolution

It is over a year since the incident. James continues to attend school and Dwayne has returned full time. James' parents were offered mediation with the parents and carers of the other boys but declined. The boys were monitored very closely and have had little or no contact with each other since the incident. The boys are now in years 8 and 9 and both are doing very well. Dwayne has been involved in no further exclusions. James' parents have made no further complaints to the school.

This scenario raises many issues, and we are identifying four that relate to leadership.

First, this was a very tricky and heated situation where it was vital to take quick and principled action. In this case the staff and governors were fully behind the actions taken. We do not know much about the school, but it is likely that there have been previous efforts to ensure that staff and governors share the same values (there will be more discussion on this in Chapter 2). It is important that values in a school are not taken for granted and that time for reflection and discussion of values is available, particularly if there is a desire to change the culture. Structures that support equity and diversity may be helpful in altering the culture.

Second, the values of the head teacher were that all pupils had to be cared for, perhaps particularly those that are most vulnerable. Working with the social worker, the head therefore found a solution that kept Dwayne in school. His permanent exclusion from a school where he was making good progress would not have been at all helpful to his future well-being.

Third, there are very important issues of overt racism from the parents who tried to influence the wider parent body and the community. James' parents were not enthusiastic about sending him to the school in the first place, presumably because of its ethnic diversity. They tried to rally other parents from the feeder primary school to share their opinions and did their best to undermine the open evening where their son was actually assisting. They also tried to stir up feeling by contacting the press and continued to ratchet up the racial nature of the incident. It is important that governors and other stakeholders such as feeder schools, parents and the wider community see the school modeling good practice. Reputation management is difficult. As mentioned earlier, stereotypes are quick and convenient; people will easily latch on to and believe stories that support their beliefs about 'outsiders'.

Fourth, another important aspect of the incident and its management was the fact that the head teacher is from an ethnic minority and this adds another level of potential tension. The proportion of teachers from black and minority ethnic (BME) is much smaller than the proportion of students in England (Department for Education and Skills (DfES) 2006; Department for Children, Schools and Families (DCSF) 2008) and the proportion of BME head teachers is tiny (Coleman 2005). One of us undertook a small research project among BME deputy heads in London that indicate perceptions of racism and that promotion for BME senior staff may be particularly difficult in the secondary sector (Coleman and Campbell Stephens 2010).

We will now explore some of the implications for leading for diversity and social justice in education illustrated by the scenario above, starting from the point of view of the individual and their own 'critical consciousness' (Capper et al. 2006). We are increasingly aware of diversity issues for pupils and students (Lumby 2008). However, less attention has been paid to diversity among the adults who work, lead and manage within the field of education. This section of the chapter is focusing particularly on leadership for and with diversity among adults working in education.

The individual and critical consciousness

As we noted in the introduction to the chapter, it is important for leaders to be able to adopt a different lens to look at the world. Writing about racism in schooling in England, David Gillborn (2008) adopts critical race theory (CRT) to dissect the ways in which the media in England tend to place white working-class boys as 'the victims of ethnic diversity in general and race equality in particular' (Gillborn 2008: 234) because they are achieving poorly. By implication black and minority ethnic students are being 'blamed' for the poor achievement of white working-class boys. Gillborn (2008) also points out the ease with which individuals may be drawn unthinkingly by the media into classifying race as a marginal problem. A qualitative study of pre-service teachers in Australia (Santoro 2009) indicates that those who are from an Anglo-Australian background have limited understanding of other cultures despite the fact that it is a country where over 200 languages are spoken. The study found that the student teachers, and indeed their supervisors, tended to stereotype their pupils from other (non-Western) cultures, such as Vietnam or Turkey. In addition,

> The pre-service students had little awareness of their own subject positioning in relation to ethnicity. They understood 'ethnic' as a label for 'others' but not themselves. For example, Jody says in response to a question about how she understands her ethnicity: I'd always assumed that I had none.
>
> (Santoro 2009: 40)

In our research and elsewhere we have noticed that there is also a perception, particularly among younger women, that gender is no longer a discriminatory issue. However, statistics show (Equality and Human Rights Commission 2008) that there is still a 'glass ceiling' although it is possible that it has moved upwards, and there is still a substantial pay gap between men and women. At the current rate of change it will be 2225 before there are equal numbers of men and women in the boardrooms of the UK (Russell 2009: 29). The examples quoted here are about ethnicity

and gender, but a similar ignorance or downgrading of out-group characteristics can apply to any aspect of diversity.

Leaders in education may benefit from 'auditing' their own views and
encouraging and leading their staff to do the same (Begley 2003). A level
of reflection, or 'critical consciousness' (Capper et al. 2006), is important
to cut through the stereotypes and generalizations that can cloud judgement. This is particularly the case for those who are setting the ethos of
an organization. They may also draw from the diversity around them.
Discussing the leadership of multiethnic schools, Shah (2008: 530) draws
on the Muslim concept of *Adab* as a tool for leaders, arguing that this
(roughly translated as respect) 'underpins diverse aspects of relationships,
celebrates diversity, supports vulnerability, rejects discrimination (racism!)
and promotes innate human dignity'.

Reflection

Do you take time to think about your basic value stance? Do you encourage
staff to think about the values of your organization?

Changing the culture

Leaders in education and elsewhere have power and influence to change
the culture of the organization and to overcome cognitive and structural
barriers faced by individuals and groups in order to work towards valuing
diversity. Leaders of an organization have a particular role in changing
the culture. Leadership is closely associated with vision and values (see
Chapter 2) and managing a change in vision and values is a prime aspect
of the leader's role. We do not know how much change the head teacher in
the scenario had initiated in the school, but there was confidence that the
staff and governors were solidly behind the head teacher and it therefore
seems likely that values and vision were shared throughout the school.

In a case study of the management of change in a higher education
institution (Robertson et al. 2009: 33), the leadership team initiated the
development of 'whole staff shared understanding and ownership of a
vision of "inclusive education"'. The process took two years and was focused on three whole staff development days. The days built on each
other, and made use of external experts to draw thinking from the whole
staff rather than have change imposed from the top. It was intended to
give a sense of ownership, and all academic and administrative staff were

included: 'activities were undertaken which challenged staff to focus on their own identity/diversity, to review values and vision and to explore what [the institution] wants to say about itself regarding diversity and equality'. Over the time period there was evidence of real change which was judged successful because, although initiated from the top, the majority was 'gradually involved in co-constructing'.

One of the key findings of research carried out on successful leadership in multiethnic schools in England (Walker et al. 2005: 3) was that it is 'based on the articulation and implementation of explicit values that promote an agenda of equality, fairness and respect' and that these leaders define their leadership 'in terms of their commitment to principles of social justice'.

Integrity of values

If each individual is to be valued, it is likely that leadership will not reside solely in a person or people at the top. In the college example above, the leadership team might have initiated the discussion of inclusive education, but all staff helped develop the further days, and group leaders took responsibility for the initiative. Discussing inclusive leadership in schools, Ryan (2006: 14) states that: 'Truly inclusive leadership in education needs to run deep, ensuring that all members of the school community and their perspectives are included fairly in all school processes.' Inclusive leadership is illustrated by the head teacher's action in the scenario, where the view is taken that all those in the school deserve the same consideration.

The ethos and values endorsed by the leaders of an organization have been shown to have an impact on diversity. In respect of employees with disabilities, Stone and Collela (1996) have identified the values that help or hinder the employment of potentially disadvantaged employees:

> In particular we believe that the values associated with competitive achievement, rugged individualism, self-reliance, in-group superiority, or conformity in appearance may negatively affect the degree to which disabled individuals are viewed as qualified for jobs. However, when organizations value social justice, egalitarianism, and engender norms of cooperation and helpfulness, disabled individuals should be viewed as more suitable for jobs and more capable of making contributions to the organization.
> (Stone and Collela 1996: 373)

Just as equal opportunities legislation is necessary if not sufficient to bring about a change in culture, structural changes within an institution can help to underpin a change and set an ethos that is helpful in ensuring that everyone is conscious of the issues relating to diversity.

Useful structures

Policies relating to diversity and social justice often relate to students rather than staff in higher education (Deem and Morley 2006). However, there is evidence of a growing positive effort relating to diversity in the sector. In some cases diversity is central to the ethos in higher education. As part of a recent research project, one of us received this statement from a senior university figure:

> We concentrate on diversity. Everyone has diversity training and induction. This includes awareness of family responsibilities, and religious differences. We monitor the statistics for gender, ethnicity, disabilities and have targets. We look at all advertisements for jobs, and at interviews and other types of assessment, to ensure they are diversity friendly. We have a strong flexible employment policy. We have a special initiative to encourage women in to the professoriate. For senior positions we make efforts to seek out a diverse range of applicants. The application processes are checked to ensure that they will bring out the best in the applicants.
>
> (Coleman, previously unpublished data)

The structures mentioned in this extract help to ensure that the vision and values that are so vital can be carried through in practice:

- Diversity *training* and induction
- Having clear *targets* for diversity
- *Monitoring* of the targets
- *Checking* wording of advertisements
- *Checking* interviews and other forms of assessment
- *Flexibility* for those with family responsibilities
- Making *efforts to attract* diverse candidates for senior positions.

A policy on equality and diversity would include careful monitoring of all recruitment and appointments and take a proactive stance towards those groups and individuals who may have been overlooked or penalized in the past.

Reflection

What does your institutional policy on diversity and equality cover? Might there be useful additions?

Professional development

A day spent considering the values of an organization or a day on the development of a diversity policy could be the focus of a programme of staff development. This could also form the basis for mainstreaming diversity; that is, putting it as central to all aspects of policy and practice in the institution.

As in the case of the higher education institution mentioned above (Robertson et al. 2009) professional development in the form of training days should be inclusive not only of all staff, academic and administrative, but of the governors, who often act as gatekeepers when they recruit and interview prospective senior staff. My research with both women and BME staff has indicated that governors tend to be particularly stereotypical in their views about leaders (Coleman 2005; Coleman and Campbell Stephens 2009).

In addition to organizing professional development focusing on understanding and valuing diversity for all staff, there is the possibility of organizing professional development specifically for potentially marginalized groups. For example there could be a women's network, or leadership courses specifically for women or ethnic minorities. Women who belong to women-only groups enjoy and benefit from the freedom of single-sex gatherings. In research one of us did with a group of women secondary head teachers, not only was the group a source of professional support and development but also:

> We could meet and let our hair down, say 'how do we cope with this?' We could not do that in a mixed group. Men would appear to have the answers even though they did not.
>
> (Coleman 2009a: 9)

The leadership course 'Investing in Diversity' that has operated in London for several years draws its members from BME teaching staff in schools. When we undertook an in-depth evaluation of the course (Coleman and Campbell Stephens 2009) we found that the participants were often adamant that they do not want positive discrimination. Despite this, the participants rate highly the benefits of a BME-only course because they can compare experiences. Typical comments on what was best about the course include the following:

- Meeting colleagues who understand the issues of being a black leader.
- Being able to have honest discussions knowing that they are confidential.
- Experiencing trust and support.

Mentoring and role models

Mentoring is a particularly useful form of professional development, not only as part of an induction for new recruits to teaching or any other profession, but also as part of an induction for promoted posts. It is discussed further in Chapter 11. It can be used for supporting individuals who face the additional difficulties of overcoming stereotypes and prejudice.

Mentoring includes many functions. Initially these might include providing a safe listening ear and offering support with problems. Once the mentee has begun to settle in, mentors can act as coaches, providing a more challenging type of support as the mentee grows into the job and the pair get to know and trust each other more. Although mentoring is highly valued, there can be problems. These are mainly to do with matching mentor and mentee, ensuring that mentors have appropriate training, and then giving sufficient time for the relationship to be useful. Where people are coming from diverse backgrounds, pairing will need particular attention. Some individuals may feel happier being mentored by someone who shares the same background as them, but this is not always achievable since senior people tend to be those of the 'insider group'. In fact mentoring of an 'out-group' individual by someone from the in-group may have benefit. Some women have spoken highly of being championed by men, as the men are likely to have more contacts, influence and power than women. Nevertheless, where mentoring of 'outsiders' is undertaken by members of the in-group, there may be additional problems. Ragins (2002) identifies challenges where the ethnicity or the gender of the mentor and mentee are different. Some of the issues relate to sensitivity about the use of stereotypes, and difficulties with the pairs feeling comfortable in talking about diversity issues. Strategies to deal with such difficulties include the use of role modelling, and attending diversity training and consciousness-raising sessions together. It was found that while some pairs managed the relationship by absolute avoidance of diversity issues, others took an approach of active confrontation. The most important strategy that the pairs adopted was clarifying the ground rules under which they operated.

An innovative way of 'reverse' mentoring that focuses on diversity has been adopted in a commercial environment where a senior person who is aiming to be inclusive is mentored by a younger person who is an 'outsider' in some way (Ian Dodds Consulting 2006). The senior person who is the mentee in this case is then coached by the more junior mentor, who can suggest how the leader can work even more successfully with and for diversity.

Resources may mean that formal mentoring cannot be offered, but the simple device of ensuring that there are diverse role models has a very powerful effect. In the following examples taken from research that one of us undertook in 2008, simply seeing role models who were of the same ethnicity enabled two BME women teachers to aspire to promotion:

> [I] saw that the deputy head at her daughter's school was black and thought: 'If she can do it I would love to do it too', she was a positive role model and this led me into teaching.

Similarly:

> In my second school we had OFSTED and the inspector was a black lady, and that inspired me. She did not say anything to me, but seeing her as a professional black woman inspired me to do more.
>
> (Coleman and Campbell Stephens 2009: 30)

In a study of an all-women network of secondary head teachers (Coleman 2009b: 4) the women heads ensured that they had equal opportunities in their own schools. They talked about 'bringing on' women. By this they did not mean affirmative action but the application of equal opportunities so that women were considered for roles where they had previously been excluded. One of the women stated: 'If we could not do it [develop female leadership] we cannot expect males to do it.' She went on to say:

> When I took over the headship you had to go down the rankings 15 places to find a senior woman in the school. . . . It was about 50/50 men and women, but all the promoted posts were male and all the teaching staff and support staff except for technicians were women. Now we have a balance on everything.

This approach is an example of how it is possible to model good practice to the institution and to the wider community.

Reflection

Is attention given to the impact of role models in your institution?

Modelling good practice and reputation management

In the scenario that provides the illustration for this chapter, you sense how the action of a few parents could have an inordinate effect on the reputation of the school. Working with parents is notoriously difficult. Harris and Goodall (2008: 286) point out that: 'parental engagement increases with social status, income and parents' level of education' and that 'differential strategies are needed to secure the engagement of a diverse range of parents'. However, the same research concluded that there comes a point where disproportionate efforts to reach a small hard core of parents who were resistant to coming into school were probably not worth it, and that the effort was better put into working with those parents who are already engaged. Ryan (2006), writing about Canada and England, points out the importance of not being too confrontational about issues like combating racism as it can create resistance and anger:

> The best route to take, then, is one that is positive without allowing people to be too comfortable with themselves and that prompts them to reflect on the present state of affairs but doesn't produce the fear and guilt that trigger further conflict. This strategy recognizes that people make mistakes and that these mistakes should be acknowledged and discussed in a constructive manner.
> (Ryan 2006: 112)

It would be possible for the local press to blow up an incident such as that reported in the scenario and to misrepresent what had actually happened. The local feeder schools and their parents need to understand what the issues are and to be clear about their motives for choosing a secondary school for their children. Foskett and Hemsley-Brown (1999) identify two sorts of communications between a school or college and the wider community. One is 'sales communication' concerned with the recruitment of students or pupils. The other is 'relationship communication' concerned with media relations, alumni associations, parent teacher associations and newsletters.

The more that a school or other educational institution has integrated its values into the thinking of staff, students, governors and parents, the easier it will be to ensure that a united front is presented to those who are outside the immediate boundaries. For example Foskett and Hemsley-Brown (1999: 222) identify the fives Cs: 'consistency, clarity, concern, cooperation and confidence as key components of the interface between the institution and the community'. It is important that individuals or groups are identified who will take responsibility for fostering relationships with the wider community including businesses, feeder institutions and the media so that there is a clear channel of communication at all times, but particularly when there is a newsworthy incident.

As the scenario illustrates, where BME candidates hold high profile roles, care in the relationship with the community and the media may be particularly necessary.

Diversity and educational leaders

Educational leaders do not represent the diversity that might be found among students and pupils and the community as a whole. Even in primary schools where the majority of head teachers are women, men are proportionately more likely to become a head. Outside the large conurbations, women are very much in the minority in leadership positions in secondary schools (Fuller 2009). The proportion of leaders from a BME background or who have any form of disability is very small (Coleman 2005). Issues such as sexual orientation rarely surface and are regarded as extremely sensitive (Lugg and Tooms 2010). Those who can be visibly identified with a religious faith, for example some Muslims, find that they may be excluded from promotion (Shah and Shaikh 2010). Research with BME leaders in England in schools and colleges (McKenley and Gordon 2002; Bush et al. 2005, 2006; Mackay and Etienne 2006; Coleman and Campbell Stephens 2010) has shown that there is an undercurrent of racism which impedes career progress.

Given these circumstances it is particularly important that leadership training includes training for social justice and awareness of diversity issues. In a wide-ranging review of the leadership training for head teachers in England, Brundrett and Anderson de Cuevas (2008) identify as a key concern:

> A re-examination of the curriculum content of leadership preparation programmes to ensure that key topics are included that assist school leaders in developing the reflective consciousness, knowledge and skill sets required to lead on issues of social justice.
>
> (Brundrett and Anderson de Cuevas 2008: 258)

Summary

In this chapter we have stressed the need for a conscious consideration of and reflection on the values adopted by individuals towards issues of diversity, stereotyping and discrimination. Within an approach that values individuals equally it should be possible not only to eliminate discrimination but to value the diversity of the individuals and their contribution to the organization.

The main issues that were considered in this chapter were the promotion of equality and valuing of diversity through:

- Having regular discussions of values
- Establishing understanding among the stakeholders
- Establishing a policy and other structures to support diversity
- Using professional development for all and consideration of focused professional development for specific groups
- Recognizing the importance of mentoring and role models
- Modelling good practice to the community
- Implementing reputation management
- Acknowledging the importance of including social justice issues in training for educational leaders.

The issues of diversity and social justice underpin what you will be reading in the rest of the book.

Further reading

For more about the theory and practice of leadership and diversity take a look at: Lumby, J. with Coleman, M. (2008) *Leadership and Diversity: Challenging Theory and Practice in Education*. London: Sage.

A clear account drawing on practice mainly in Canada: Ryan, J. (2006) *Inclusive Leadership*. San Francisco, CA: Jossey-Bass.

2   Leading with values

Anne Gold

In an educational organization, why are values important in underpinning leadership actions and decisions? How might clear leadership values lead to principled decision-making? What happens when values conflict? How might conflicting values be brought towards agreed outcomes that satisfy everyone concerned? Do all 'good' educational leaders hold the same values? How are the articulation and transparency of leadership values possible? In what other ways might clear leadership values help a leader to respond *well* to the challenges of working in an educational organization?

In this chapter and the book as a whole, discussions about values are illustrated within a framework of social justice and democracy. Within this framework, it is taken for granted that an underpinning value such as 'fairness' leads to a form of social justice that relies on democracy to develop and support it. Such a political and social way of organizing civil life is taken for granted in many countries, but it may be seen as a luxury in others and feared or mistrusted in yet others. We recognize therefore that some of our assumptions about the 'best' way of leading educational organizations might be seen as Western or anglophone, but this is the academic and scholarly paradigm within which we work.

The chapter begins with some quotations about values and educational leadership in order to set out some of the current discussions. There follows an example of a situation in which several people who have leadership responsibility and share an equally strong commitment to the well-being of an educational organization hold conflicting views. This illustration is drawn from many years' experience as a school teacher, a university teacher, a researcher and a school governor. Although it takes place in a very English school, bounded by English education laws, and appearing to rely on very British ways of negotiating (or not) a lack of consensus, we believe that it shows some universal and important dilemmas and discussion points.

In this case, the organization is a large secondary school, but the issues raised in the discussion could be linked with any educational organization. The conflict means that a set of school leaders are unable to agree on a key appointment to the organization. We suggest strategies for avoiding the conflict, and we ask questions about the responsibility for resolving the issue, or for making sure that it did not occur initially. Some suggestions are made about strategies for articulating, exploring and revisiting a leader's underpinning principles.

Research about leadership and values is then introduced. The research shows that clearly articulated values are more easily communicated to an educational community and would thus ultimately lead to the construction of a shared sense of direction.

The chapter ends with suggestions about three leadership activities on which educational leaders might reflect. Their linkage to values is not initially apparent although they are clearly values based. They are common sites where values are displayed to the educational community – they are part of the everyday task of educational leadership.

Some thoughts and definitions about values in educational leadership

First, here is a definition indicating our stance on values, one which is commonly although not universally adopted:

> I take 'values' to signify the core beliefs about life and about relating to other people that underpin understandings, principles and ethics about education, and here, about the leadership of education... the key set of values that drives the decisions of a school leader is concern with an understanding of the nature of power relations. Empowerment, democracy, equity and inclusion are all linked with power distribution and all depend on values and relationships.
>
> (Gold 2004: 3)

Here are some more thoughts about values and educational leadership: this is a short selection of ideas from a large body of writing on the subject – the quotations are by way of an introduction to the field.

> Those educational leaders who take the opportunity to articulate their own values about education and about leadership in education despite the tumult surrounding education at the moment in several countries, are likely to make better informed and more profoundly professional decisions. Clearly articulated values leave a leader less likely to vacillate between different political and educational orthodoxies and more able to respond thoughtfully.
>
> (Gold 2004: 6)

Hodgkinson (1991), a highly respected Canadian writer on the philosophy of education, wrote:

> Administration or leadership in its fullest sense is more concerned with values than with facts ... the facts can *never* be in conflict while the values, assuming there are more than one set, are *always* in conflict.
>
> (Hodgkinson 1991: 89, original emphases)

Values underpin leadership:

> All leaders consciously or unconsciously employ values as guides to interpreting situations and suggesting appropriate action. This is the artistry of leadership.
>
> (Begley 2003: 11)

We are all concerned with values:

> 'Values' is not a technical term. In talking about values, we are talking about something that is part of the experience of everyone.
>
> (Haydon 2007: 6)

Haydon (2007) then goes on to offer a strategy for his reader to think about and articulate their values about education, taking them through a chain of questions and answers which direct them to their underpinning values.

These fragments about values and leadership in education serve to set the scene for this chapter. They show how values are implicit in all of us, that they are different in all of us, that they are difficult to articulate but that they are fundamental to everything we do. They guide every decision we make, even if we are not aware of this.

Now let us consider a practical example of a conflict of values.

Scenario: Conflicting values in an English school

The task

The school in question has recently began to receive additional funding (from central government) to become a specialist school with a focus on the performing arts. A selection panel has been drawn up to choose the key post of Head of the Performing Arts Faculty. The successful appointee will support and advise the leadership team in leading the school through to this enhanced special status.

Staff selection is an important leadership duty because it provides a concrete way of ensuring that newly appointed staff members either will share a philosophy of education with the school and its leaders, or will contribute positively to its further development. The panel includes the school leader, the chair of the governing body (the school board), a teacher representative, a local authority representative with expert knowledge about the performing arts and a governor who has been chosen by the parents to represent them. Although not all the panel members are directly or paid leaders of the school, this exercise is one which calls for leadership qualities and responsibilities because of the importance of a correct appointment. All of the interviewers will have attended a local course on equal opportunities interviewing, at which they will have been asked to think about issues of diversity and they will have been inducted into an agreed selection procedure.

Their first task was to agree a shortlist of applicants who were then to be interviewed by the panel. In accordance with the selection policy to which they were introduced in their training, everyone on their shortlist fits the person specification and has the right qualifications and professional experience to be offered the post – the interview is taking place to choose the best person to suit the school from the agreed shortlist.

The shortlist

Their agreed shortlist contains three excellent candidates:

Henry is a 45-year-old former actor who has retrained as a teacher and who has been teaching for five years. He has enormous charisma and wide personal contacts in the professional field of performance. He would bring energy and a deep and personal understanding of performance arts, as well as links to useful sponsors and insider knowledge of many performance spaces and professional demands.

Sarah is a 33-year-old energetic, bright, committed teacher. She has superb qualifications and professional experience, both in performance and in education and she has a Master's degree in educational leadership. She would bring energy, charm and tact as well as both a practical and a theoretical understanding of performance, education and educational leadership.

Claire is a stylish and articulate 57-year-old woman who has worked her way through several schools as a music teacher, a head of a music department and a pastoral head in schools and colleges of further education. She appears calm and purposeful about the challenges this post will bring – she has already responded successfully and creatively to several such challenges in her career. She brings experience and success in managing change as well as the respect of all those with whom she has worked previously.

The conflict

It is clear even before the interview that, unusually for the school, they could appoint any one of the three candidates – they are all capable in different ways of helping to take the school forward. In the interviews, all three are impressive. Henry's expertise in performance and his wide contacts would clearly be very useful to the school, but the brevity of his experience in education and the charisma that everyone found so attractive could mean that the teaching staff might find it hard to regard him as a senior and responsible teacher.

Sarah shows that the depth of her subject knowledge, her sense of humour and her clear integrity would make her a powerful middle leader. She demonstrates her knowledge and expertise of teaching, performing and leading others during the course of the interview and she is by far the most inspiring candidate of the three. She would 'fit' exactly into the role that was vacant. In response to a final question about accommodation because she would have to move nearer to the school if she were offered the post, she tells the panel that she is newly married and would be looking for a suitable house to buy.

Claire shows that she could be relied on to manage the change carefully and thoroughly. She is used to such challenges and would inspire confidence in those with whom she worked. Her advice would obviously be sound and worthwhile, but perhaps it would not be risk-taking and energetic enough. There was some unspoken sense that she might be too near retirement to give the school many years of service, but clearly she has wisdom in abundance.

The selection panel cannot agree about the right person to employ: the chair of governors wants to offer the post to Claire as a 'safe pair of hands' – the school is going through such profound change that she wants to appoint someone who would be respected and reliable. She thinks Henry does not know enough about the leadership of schools and she is worried that Sarah, because of her recent marriage, would be asking for maternity leave within a year or two of her appointment.

The teacher representative is excited by Sarah's experience, skills, energy and integrity. She thinks the threat of maternity leave is an unlawful distraction, and she would dearly like to work with Sarah.

The local authority representative votes for Henry because his connections and his charisma would mean that he could raise important funding and he could connect with and impress local and national performance companies and sponsors. He can find no really negative points for either

Sarah or Claire, but he is very positive about the possibilities of Henry's contributions to the school.

The parent representative is absolutely sure that Claire is the best candidate. His daughter had been in a class the previous year which had been taught by three different maths teachers within the year, because of the promotion to a new and senior post of the first teacher and the maternity leave of the second teacher. He is looking for continuity for his daughter and it seems to him that Claire would be the safest appointment.

Although there is no outright animosity among the panel, they have reached a point where they are unable to proceed without some discomfort as several of them would have to give up their beliefs about which appointment they think would be best for the school.

The school leader is left with several dilemmas:

- She wants to employ Sarah for the same reasons as the teacher representative. Not employing her because she may become pregnant and ask for maternity leave is both against the law and a gendered decision (a newly married man would not be turned down in case he became a father), so employing Sarah is a risk she is prepared to take. She does not think that either Henry or Claire could make such valuable and focused contributions to the development of the school as Sarah.
- But as the school leader, she does not want to impose her will on the others. She is aware of the effect of power relations within the hierarchy of such organizations as schools, and she wants to be respectful of all panel members' views; she is uncomfortable about using her status to force them into agreeing with her. They each have valid and thoughtful suggestions to make and she values their responses as representing the different dynamic constituents of this successful school.
- Ideally she would like the panel to have an informed discussion that addressed all the issues raised but which would then still come to the conclusion she could best support and use most constructively in the development of the school.
- She is a democratic leader at heart and would prefer a meeting which, unless it could agree unanimously, could take a vote and abide by the outcome – even if the outcome is against the original wishes of members of the meeting. In this case, she may have to give up her preferred candidate because as there is no outright majority vote for Sarah.

There are two conceptualizations which might help explain some of these dilemmas. First, Woods (2005: 32) writes about democratic leadership to show how important it is because it is 'integral to a good society and, in consequence, is intimately bound with education'. His work would support the school leader here as she emphasizes that the decisions should be reached through democratic processes: in a democratic society, democratic decision-making, underpinned by fairness, takes place at all levels and affects all other levels. One of the most important places it is learnt is in the school.

Second, Begley (2004: 16) has a useful theory about the sources of values and value conflict when he describes the arenas of administration (or leadership). The school leader in the example above is dealing with several values conflicts at different levels, or arenas – the individual or personal level; the organizational level and the community level:

> Thinking in terms of the arenas of administration serves two important functions. It suggests the various sources of values, conveying how values can be derived from multiple external and internal environmental sources in dynamic ways. The notion of arenas also conveys the potential sources of value conflicts. For example, although value conflicts can certainly occur within a single arena of administration, consider how the personal values of the individual might conflict with those of the community, or professional values might conflict with organizational values.
>
> (Begley 2004: 16)

In the scenario, the school leader is struggling with dilemmas not only about the appointment itself but also about her leadership of the school, and about her preference for a specific candidate as well as her wish that every panel member should contribute to the decision-making.

The values conflicts

Each panel member is making a serious and values-led choice about their preferred appointee:

- The parent representative is thinking about the well-being of his daughter – being a good parent, he is supporting his own child in the best way he can.
- The local authority representative, in keeping with a 'new managerialist' discourse, may be influenced by the promise of money and prestige that Henry may bring to the school – he is persuaded by the government's agenda about 'value for money' that encourages educational organizations to be as financially independent as possible.

- Some panel members are thinking about the stability and comfort of all the young people in the school in general so that they will achieve the most in life.
- Some are focused on the best creative development of the whole school curriculum – they bring profound professional values into the discussion.
- Others are paying attention to fairness through such diversity issues as:
  - *Age* – in the preference for or against Claire.
  - *Class* (as played out in previous qualifications and experience) – in the respect given to Sarah with her excellent professional qualifications.
  - But ultimately this appears to be about *gender*, which is shown in a discussion about how one woman's potential reproductive activity could disrupt the education of many young people.
- The school leader is also deeply concerned with fairness, through her view of democracy and her commitment to ethical decision-making while taking responsibility for the key activity of the school – effective learning and teaching.

In this way, there are values conflicts between the panel members and internally within some of the members themselves. The school leader is a good example of internal values conflict – her deeply held values about fairness bring her into a conflict between her wish to be a transparent and democratic leader and her desire for social justice. Her commitment to fairness underpins both her beliefs about democracy and her quest for social justice, but those two sets of beliefs are in opposition here because her most deeply held belief is about fairness. Based on this underpinning principle, she has developed her understandings about democracy and social justice: they spring from her struggle to be as fair as possible, but here they conflict. If she were truly committed to democratic decision-making, she would rely on a vote which might ultimately give the job to someone (Henry or Claire) who would not fit with her understandings about social justice. And if she allowed her understandings about social justice to prevail, she would have to manipulate the decision-making processes undemocratically in order to be able to offer the post to Sarah.

Reflection

If you think carefully about the principles underpinning your own professional life, can you find any conflicting values? If so how do you resolve this conflict?

This conflict might have been avoided, or at least worked through to an agreement more easily, if everyone in the panel had a clear understanding of the values that underpinned the new direction of the school. The decision may have been easier if the whole school community had agreed together a philosophy of education that made direct links with the new performing arts specialism to which the school is working.

The importance of clearly articulated values

How would more clearly articulated and shared values have forestalled this clash of values? If the educational leader's values (about democratic leadership, about social justice and about the energy and creativity she wanted to foster in the school) were known and ultimately shared by the whole school community before the selection procedure, would this selection procedure have gone more smoothly?

As Haydon (2007) writes:

> If a principal says that her school is a community ... she is probably not making a neutral sociological observation (which would be true of any school), but means to convey a positive evaluation: saying that the school has some desirable features that would not be shared by just any school.
>
> (Haydon 2007: 93)

So in the case of the school above, the 'desirable features' will, of course, include continuity, first-rate learning and teaching and social justice (the primary values of some members of the panel), but also, because as its chosen specialism, the school is moving towards excelling in the performing arts, it is looking for leadership and expertise in that area.

There are several good texts on the management of change in educational organizations. One useful book which looks at the complexity of change at both macro and micro levels is by Morrison (1998). In accordance with such texts, and in order to change direction effectively, a well-led school community will have completed some apparently time-consuming preparatory work to bring them to this selection panel. Although they may not have been in the following order, these stages will have been passed through:

- A need for a fundamental change in the direction of the school will have become apparent to the school leader.
- The school leader will have put forward a tentative proposal about the change to either the senior leadership team or the governors' (school board) meeting. The proposal will probably include the

results of a mapping exercise to show how possible the change is, some planning stages and possible outcomes.

- If she does not attain general support after providing evidence and plans, she will probably not go ahead because she will know that the community is not ready for her ideas. Or she will work further on preparing the readiness of her senior team for change.
- Having attained the goodwill and support of the first meeting she will put the proposal, with added suggestions from that meeting, to the other key leadership team (the senior leadership team or the governors' meeting – whichever she did not present it to in the first place). And she will listen to *their* suggestions and make relevant amendments.
- With the support of both key leadership teams, she will call a whole staff meeting where she will describe her plans and lay before them a process which will allow all staff to discuss and make suggestions for better implementation.
- At this stage, the school leader and her teams will make suggestions, listen to responses, set up appropriate working parties and engage in many 'learning conversations' (Brookfield 1987), where they will learn as much as the person to whom they are talking. This is the stage where the leader builds in both the voices of her staff and their agreement and compliance with the change in the organization's educational direction. We know that this school leader places her belief in democracy and democratic leadership high in her values system. Because of her sense of fairness (and her belief that those people she works with are energetic and committed professionals) she sets off a process which encourages feedback and suggestions from the staff and in which they all learn – they work in Freireian 'dialoguing' (Freire 1970) – and eventually from the whole community, a set of plans emerge that will lead the organization towards a dynamic and creative change.
- So the values that underpin the change in direction of the organization will include those that foster dynamism, creativity and energy. The job description for the person to lead the school through this change – the Head of the Performing Arts Faculty – will include these terms and the applicant will need to portray them.
- Only Sarah displayed these qualities in her application and at interview. So she most closely fitted the values and direction of the organization.

The school leader may not have chaired or even been present at all the meetings – her leadership values may well have led her to work through a distributed leadership style (Leithwood et al. 2009) – but she will have made sure that the process was effective. If she has led the organization through this long but educative process in an articulate and transparent way in accordance with her values about democracy and her understanding about power and knowledge, she will be able to point towards the agreed qualities in the discussion after the interview. Although initially some members of the panel may be influenced by their own agendas, there will be commitment to the change in the school's direction and a reminder of this will (it is hoped) bring them to a unanimous vote for Sarah.

In an earlier book, Leithwood (1999) described such leaders as 'transformational'. They are people who:

- More adequately anticipate many of the constraints likely to arise during problem solving.
- Show a greater tendency to plan, in advance, for how to address anticipated constraints.
- Respond more adaptively and flexibly to constraints that arise unexpectedly.
- Do not view constraints as major impediments to problem-solving.

(Leithwood 1999: 104)

It may be that some educational leaders, when presented with the necessity to make speedy and important decisions, are convinced that they can best do so alone. This example of shared values and shared decision-making is offered in order to persuade readers of the basic worth and virtue of such shared practices. They demand time for reflection, for planning and for working with an educational community. There are suggestions for ensuring such time for reflection later in this chapter.

Research findings

Throughout the description of the decision-making processes above, there is a recurrent theme of the importance of the clear articulation and communication of leadership values. I was involved in two research projects which explored ways in which leaders articulate those values and, in the case of the second piece, how they were seen by their professional communities.

In the first piece of research (Campbell et al. 2003), some school leaders were asked about the links between their values and their leadership styles, about the values that informed their school culture, about the extent to which their values affected the school culture, about how they were influenced by their local community (not the school community) and about how much they thought the school's values affected the students inside and outside the classroom. This was a piece of small-scale research and the answers to our questions were not triangulated by discussions with those they led; we wanted to hear what the school leaders themselves thought rather than what others thought about them.

We were struck by the fact that although the leaders to whom we spoke had quite widely differing values which underpinned their leadership practice, we could see that they all described their values as being influential in what they wanted for the young people in their schools, for their leadership of their staff and how they managed relationships with the community in and around the school. We saw that:

> In very different ways the head teachers held strong values which informed their leadership, taking responsibilities, maintaining oversight, making difficult decisions if required and driving change when necessary. They all appeared to be combining strong but different styles of leadership with democratic values and a commitment to working with the school and community, in a continuum which ranges from some educational leadership activities as public relations issues to changing the way the young people and therefore the whole community, relate to each other.
>
> (Campbell et al. 2003: 220)

Thus, although there was a marked difference in these leaders' values and in the ways they led their organizations, they could all articulate their values clearly to us. And they told us that these values profoundly affected all their leadership decisions and activities.

The second research project in which I was involved (Gold et al. 2003) was based on ten case studies of highly rated (by both government and local authority inspectors) educational leaders. We carried out these case studies within a much larger research project about school leadership and although we did not ask about leadership values directly, as we wrote up our findings from the case studies, we could see that these outstanding leaders were all:

> undoubtedly translating their educational values into leadership practices.
>
> As researchers *we* were able to make clear connections between the school leaders' values and their leadership, and they did often tell us about the schools' strong and shared value systems. ... We were intrigued by the ways they worked to build these shared values. ... In essence, we found that they all worked towards articulating and communicating values by:
>
> - Working with, managing and even searching out change
> - Keeping staff constantly informed

- Working closely with their senior management and leadership teams
- Developing leadership capacity and responsibility throughout the school.

These four main strategies (shared by all our case study schools) were the clearest examples of leadership in action which led us to describe the values of the leaders to whom we spoke. We took them as both indicators and implementers of underpinning leadership values.

(Gold 2004: 11–12)

Both pieces of research linked leadership, values and education to show that whatever values led educational leaders into working in education and then into leading educational organizations, they also affected and influenced the ways in which these people lead the other people in their organizations. Taking both sets of research together, the cross section of educational leaders interviewed represented several very different belief systems – some led faith schools, some led large inner-city secondary schools, some led small special schools and others led small rural primary schools. But they all displayed their values clearly in many different ways, and those who worked with them (and those who researched them) were able to 'read' those values and to link them to their professional duties and to the school culture and future direction.

Reflection

When you think about the educational leaders with whom you are working at present, can you 'read' their values in their actions? And indeed, which of your values can be read in your own actions?

Maintaining leadership values

When we wrote about the findings of the second research project described above (Gold et al. 2003), we suggested that the educational leaders:

Were principled individuals with a strong commitment to their 'mission', determined to do the best for their schools, particularly for the pupils and students within them. They endeavoured to mediate the many externally driven directives to ensure, as far as it was possible, that their take-up was consistent with what the school was trying to achieve.

(Gold et al. 2003: 136)

We wrote that their values helped them to make leadership decisions which picked a principled path through the multiplicity of external demands in order to link the chosen direction of the school to the best interests of the school community.

This view was critiqued by Wright (2003: 142), who considered that we had not taken enough account of the way that there has been 'a subtle capturing of the leadership discourse' into such discourses as the managerialist one, developed and fed in the UK by the government partly by setting up an organization such as the National College for School Leadership (now the National College for Leadership of Schools and Children's Services) and by the expansion of the National Professional Qualifications for Headship. As Ball (2008: 140) writes, 'Leadership has become a generic mechanism for change as well as a new kind of subject position within policy.'

Wright (2003) is correct in suggesting that some educational leaders could become people who respond to external demands without interrogating them thoroughly enough and thus ultimately delivering their managerialist tasks in ways that do not fit their values, or that subtly change their values. However, most principled educational leaders develop strategies that allow them space and opportunities to measure up such demands against their values and principles.

Below are some suggested strategies for such space and opportunities.

- Develop strategies to recognize and understand dominant discourses about leadership of a diverse community.
- Ensure space is set up in which to measure these discourses against their own central personal values about how to relate to other people and about leading in education.
- Embed opportunities to develop systems, underpinned by strong principles, which sustain the vision, while continuing to respond where necessary to external demands on leaders in education.

There are links here with the discussion of critical consciousness in Chapter 1. People working in different cultures and in different settings may well add to these suggestions – they are quite dependent on a culture of discussion and an informal power balance. The list depends on musing, talking, discussing and taking precious time before coming to final conclusions. I suggest that leaders set up practical strategies for reflection on values which include the following:

- Being mentored, mentoring others or mentoring oneself
- Reflective writing
- The 'Five Whys'.

Being mentored, mentoring others or mentoring oneself

I am aware that mentoring schemes in different parts of the world are based on fundamentally different assumptions about the role and nature of mentoring. The key point here, underpinning all the suggestions on my list, is the necessity to look for the opportunity to reach through layers of action and response to get to underpinning values. These opportunities are best found in safe and wise discussions with others as in the mentoring relationship. When that is not available, it is necessary to develop strategies which simulate a dialogue, although they could occur within one person.

Reflective writing

As our research showed, educational leaders are not always in clear touch with their underpinning values about learning and teaching and about leading learning and teaching, even if those around them can 'see' them. And indeed, Wright (2003) argues that these values may shift or are captured by the current political and educational discourses in which they live. So articulating and acknowledging the influences of the values is especially important. In the absence of anyone else to discuss such issues with, a reflective diary or journal can offer the distance and space for reflection that allow for such clarification.

The 'Five Whys'

One way of getting to basic principles is to ask the 'Five Whys'. This means that each time we need to think about or explain an action, we ask 'why' then 'why' again, about five times. Each time we ask 'why' we reach a deeper stage of explanation until we cannot ask any more. Then we will have reached the underpinning principle, attached to a value. It is useful to do this activity whenever new organizational rules are developed – for example, when deciding whether to set up agreed organizational guidelines on the frequency of marking or commenting on drafts of writing. A decision which may originally have been based on teachers' preferred pattern may change as the underpinning principles of good teaching, underpinned by fairness become clearer in answering the 'whys'.

There are many other ways of making sure a leader has the peace and space to be able to reach profound and worthwhile conclusions, and these will differ according to culture, history and personality. It is necessary to be reminded of these strategies, so that leadership actions flow from values and are considered and worthwhile.

Leadership in education

Having worked through a practical example of a conflict of values I have argued about the importance of the clarity of leadership values. Such clarity, although it is difficult to achieve, will inform all leadership decisions and actions. They also set a culture for an organization in which everyone strives for transparency and clarity.

There are many other leadership activities which are more effectively completed by a leader who talks regularly to staff and who is thoughtful and values-led. Below, are just a few which illustrate this point. They involve a leadership dimension which is especially pertinent to those who work in education. They are issues that underpin effective learning and which also display leadership values. They make the difference, I believe, between administering an organization and planning for profound change of direction. My research and teaching led me to think that it is up to the leader to ensure that there are constant opportunities for 'learning' conversations so that attention would be paid to the following learning challenges:

- Responsibility
- Boundaries
- Modelling values.

Responsibility

By responsibility, I mean that delicate balance between imposing blame and developing conscientious dependability. This is a moral and values-informed balance which determines the level of development in learners and teachers alike in order to make informed decisions. In other words, the amount of responsibility given to teachers and to learners throughout their time in a place of education over their own actions is a highly developmental choice to be made by the educative leader. It encompasses actions within self (such as completing learning tasks satisfactorily and without punishment), actions between self and others (such as showing respect for others and not imposing upon their learning spaces) and actions and thoughts entirely for other people (such as the development of altruistic activities such as giving to charity and trying to make a difference in the wider society).

Boundaries

Respect for boundaries is one of the first lessons I learned as a young teacher. By this I mean clarity about the space between people within the organization, so that there is safety from which to take risks but also knowledge about when those risks may do damage – knowing when the space is too big. In other words, learners and teachers need a clear working map about what they can expect from each other in order to develop effective learning and teaching. This map may be in the form of organizational rules, guidelines, roles, expectations or responsibilities. The name chosen for the boundaries is significant because it signifies the power balance that the organization is building between learners and teachers. When moving from one organization to another, the strength and distance of boundaries can be seen to be profoundly different.

Modelling values

Our research showed that even if they do not intend it to be so, teachers and leaders of teachers display their values in everything they do. We could discern values from the way others are greeted in the organization to carefully articulated attitudes to social justice. From mere and brief greetings, to who was listened to in meetings, we saw a public articulation of private thoughts. The clarity with which these values could be seen shows that teachers and their leaders are constantly modelling their beliefs to others. An important way of teaching values is to model them: if learners know that their opinions are valued, that people who are older and more powerful than them listen to what they say, those learners will then listen to others who are even less powerful than themselves.

Summary

This chapter, continuing from the first, expands on the importance of reflection on values for educational leaders. It shows how easily values clashes can lead to difficult dilemmas in an educational organization. It explores, with help from literature and research, the visibility, importance of clear articulation and strategies for sharing communal values. And it offers educational leaders some ways of planning for reflection as well as suggesting some unexpected sites of visible display of leadership values.

Further reading

For more about the practice of leadership with values read: Gold, A. (2004) *Values and Leadership*. London: Institute of Education, University of London.

The two following books will provide further theoretical discussion of leadership and values: Haydon, G. (2007) *Values for Educational Leadership*. London: Sage.

Woods, P.A. (2005) *Democratic Leadership in Education*. London: Sage and Paul Chapman.

3   Communication

Communication into, out of and within an organization is a vital part of organizational life and the communication of values is vital in establishing the culture and the style of leadership.

Communications are between the internal stakeholders including all staff, academic and administrative, governors and the students. The ethos of the institution is also communicated to a range of external stakeholders, those who visit the school or college on a regular basis and those who may only receive written communication, or attend open days and public meetings. Perhaps the most important external stakeholders of schools are parents, but schools also relate to the local or regional authority, and to businesses and other organizations in the neighbourhood as well as to the range of other services that are responsible for children's welfare. Colleges and universities also relate to their community; for example, they have important links with alumni and other potential sources of finance. All organizations have to be aware of communications with the wider world via the media and may have a dedicated member of staff or, in the case of universities, a press officer to ensure that they protect or enhance their reputation in the community.

Within the educational institution, one to one communication is also important for leaders and managers. For example, there may be mentoring and coaching of one individual of another, and one to one meetings for performance review (see Chapters 6 and 11).

Communications pervade every aspect of the leadership and management of an educational organization. In this chapter we first consider problems arising from managing communications within a complex organization and then go on to focus on the communication of values through the overall culture of the organization, the effectiveness of communications within the organization or a subgroup and then in a one to one situation. Finally we will look briefly at the impact of technology on communications in the leadership and management of education.

In any context, the structures and organizational culture may impede or facilitate clear communication as you will see in the scenario that follows.

Scenario: Communications within a UK university department

Subject departments within universities often provide examples of the problems inherent in communications. This is partly because of the complexity of relationships in large and increasingly bureaucratic institutions, and also because of the culture of professional independence maintained by the participants. The issues during one term within a small subject department in a UK university are a good example of the importance of securing good communications.

The subject department concerned had twenty-three staff led by a head of department elected for a three-year term by the staff members. This role was seen as essentially administrative, representing the departmental needs to the Dean of Faculty, the four heads of administration (finance, human resources, student welfare and research planning) and ultimately to the Vice-Chancellor. Downward communications percolated from the heads of departments via the head of subject to the other staff.

During the term in question, the second that the head of department had been in post, there were four major issues:

- The establishment of a university-wide marking policy for MA assignments.
- The possibility of securing amalgamation of three subject areas to economize on administrative time by reducing procedures replicated in all three subjects.
- The pooling of administrative and secretarial staffing so that all staff could seek help when needed and to smooth out the workloads of the currently 'individual support' assistants.
- A requirement from the head of research that there should be a move to departmental research programmes rather than the current individual interest pattern.

Looked at from the point of view of the head of department these were major matters that could not be resolved quickly and ideally would require a three-day meeting. The only time to have a meeting of that length would be during the summer vacation. Taking time during the summer vacation was resented by the staff on the grounds that it would interfere with research projects and booked holidays.

Of the twenty-three staff, seventeen agreed to spend two days at the end of the vacation looking at the issues, four said that they would make their representations during term time, and two said that they were not interested because they would be seeking early retirement in the coming year.

In the end a two-day meeting was held but it was fraught with problems. The head of department had asked the university heads of administration to lead the discussion for half a day each. This limited the time for explanation, reflection and discussion among the staff. The fact that administrators were leading the discussion was resented by some of the academics in the department. In particular the three professors within the department were intent on maintaining their own independence. As the debate proceeded they influenced others against the views of the head of department who, with her wider knowledge of what was going on in other departments, actually knew more than anyone else about what would and would not be possible.

At the end of the first day, four of the relatively junior academic staff approached the head of department and asked to be excused for the remaining day because 'we cannot feel that we are able to make any contribution – it is better for us to let it all happen and then try to fit into the new scheme'. They were persuaded to remain by the head of department who argued that 'without participation we cannot move forward and without co-operation we may be steamrollered into new arrangements that would not be to our advantage'.

The rest of the long story was built on the tensions outlined, and all four issues were resolved to the detriment of the existing subject department. The head of department reflecting on the problems recorded her thoughts as follows:

> There was too much thrust our way for debate and we had not had enough time to think things through. I allowed the professorial cabal to retain their power hold over younger staff and their research fields, and I should have allowed much more time for discussion after the administrative heads had made their presentations. In that way we might not have been seen as obstructive and we could have developed a united front to retain those things we all valued. The trouble was we never established what those were!
>
> (based on a student assignment)

Communication and management style and culture

In the scenario above there were many problems with communication that can be traced to the culture engendered by the management and leadership of the university and its departments. Throughout this book there will be references to management and leadership styles (see, for example, Chapter 8 on meetings). Three well known ideal types of management are: the collegial model where decisions are made democratically, the formal, bureaucratic model where decisions will be made by those at the top of the hierarchy, and the micro-political model typified by power struggles within the organization.

In the example of the university all three types of management are in evidence so the complexity of the organizational structure presents many opportunities for misinformation. The power relationships between the administrative heads and the academics meant that micro-political activity distorted the opportunity for open discussions (there is more discussion of micro-politics in Chapter 4). Effectively the leadership was being contested between the professors on one side and the head of department allied with the administrative heads on the other. Leonard (2001) entitles these two opposing attitudes: 'donnish dominion' versus 'managerialist'.

The university itself was hierarchical and formal in its organization with decisions being made at the top and handed down to departments to put into effect. Within the department there was an underlying lack of communication that meant that its members did not present a united front or display any ownership of the issues, with junior staff wanting to opt out of the meeting altogether. The head of department who actually knew 'more than anyone else what would and would not be possible' does not appear to have shared her knowledge fully and the department had not taken time out during the year to reflect on what they valued and the implications of that for the future.

Many leaders aspire to a collegial, collaborative style of leadership, one where open discussions lead to shared ownership of issues and decisions are arrived at through negotiation, leading to eventual consensus. In such a situation, communication would be open and honest. The leadership and management of the university and the department in the scenario are far from this ideal. Instead there is a lack of clarity about the overall strategy of the university that is driving the changes to departments. Within the department there is no time for extended meetings during term time and unwillingness on the part of staff to use vacation time for discussion about the future functioning of the department. There is no ownership on the part of the twenty-three staff in relation to the future of the department. There appears to have been no genuine discussion or negotiation and individuals did not appear to really listen to what others were saying, having taken a stance before the meeting took place.

Leaders of educational institutions have a unique opportunity to affect the culture of their organization. Prosser (1999: 8) refers to 'Predominant values embraced by an organization that determine the guiding policies and provide insiders with distinctive in-house rules for "getting on and getting by".' However, he also points out that there can be many subcultures within an organization. In the scenario above it is possible for the subculture in the department to be different from those in other departments and in the university as a whole.

The leadership of an educational organization and its sub-units will have an impact on the prevailing culture and this can be communicated in many ways. Formal communication systems can be divided into those using oral methods, such as meetings, briefing groups and public address systems, and those using the written word, such as magazines, newsletters, bulletins, notice-boards and emails; the prevailing culture may be detected from their style.

The tone of written communications such as notices, staff letters or letters to parents can convey a great deal about the nature of the organization. An example of this can be seen in the ethnographic study by Nias et al. (1989) of three primary schools, interpreting staff relationships in terms of the organizational culture. Here the written communications from two schools, one collaborative and one formal and bureaucratic, are compared:

> in the collaborative schools, notes generally had the informal quality of personal conversation:
>
>> 'I'll put the apparatus up unless anybody particularly doesn't want to use it.'
>> 'Ta very much.'
>> 'Are you free this dinnertime, Dennis, for buying plants?' (Margaret)
>>> (Extract from deputy head's Notice Book, Sedgemoor)
>
> By contrast, at Hutton, the following notes [from a staff newsletter] were more typical:
>
> General notes
>
> 1. With reference to my comment about tidiness earlier – I am becoming concerned about the general untidiness of the classrooms, particularly art areas. Children should be capable (or made to be so) of keeping areas tidy as they use them and cleaning up waste materials after themselves. Worktops should be left tidy at the end of each day so that they can be cleaned.
> 2. Please ensure that apparatus such as tape recorders is not left in classrooms overnight.

These written notices from the two schools clearly indicate contrasts in tone, culture, management and leadership style.

The culture might also be inferred from visual symbols, for example the pleasantness of the environment and the extent to which it reflects the community, and through rituals, for example the degree of formality or informality on public occasions. All of these communicate something of the ethos to the individuals working in or visiting an organization: the range of internal and external stakeholders.

> **Reflection**
>
> What would most clearly indicate the culture of your organization or department to a visitor?

A school or any other educational institution does not exist in a vacuum and will be affected by the educational policies developed by national and regional government. For example, changes towards a more target-focused system with a stress on accountability will inevitably have an impact on the ways that schools, colleges and universities operate. Also the wider national culture in which organizations operate will feed through into the institutional culture. When institutions include individuals and stakeholders from a range of cultures it is important to give thought to how communications might be received.

Communicating across cultures

No matter how clear leaders and managers might be about messages that they are trying to communicate, working with multicultural stakeholders raises complex issues about communication. Blandford and Shaw (2001: 158) lists examples of potential misunderstandings where the context is an international school with primarily Western ethos operating in a non-Western culture:

- Giving frank feedback in an appraisal
- Teachers encouraging students to question what they are being taught
- Delegating authority to middle managers
- Giving forthright opinions in a staff meeting.

Western educationalists would tend to encourage these four activities, as frankness, questioning and taking on authority are generally seen as desirable. This would not necessarily be the case in all cultures. In each of these situations there are potentially conflicting attitudes about the respect that individuals give to each other and difficulties where individuals with less status (students, young teachers) can be seen as questioning the authority of their seniors. All four of them challenge traditional views of power relations and acceptable ways of communicating judgements.

Such difficulties can be understood better if we refer back (see Introduction) to the cross-cultural theories of Hofstede (1991), in particular the dimension of power distance. In the case of the delegation of authority to middle managers, there may be reluctance among those who have a background of high power distance and high uncertainty avoidance to take on the responsibility of decision-taking that they normally identify with senior managers; they may feel it is disrespectful to their superiors and simply not their role. In this circumstance, Shaw (2001: 164) makes the following suggestions that might be adopted by the head teacher:

- show trust;
- encourage initiative;
- praise success;
- mentor/coach for new roles;
- structure the delegated risks to limit damage caused by errors of judgement;
- open discussion about new roles/responsibilities;
- anticipate and agree in advance what to do when things go wrong;
- develop a middle-management team identity for mutual support.

(Shaw 2001: 164)

Thomas (2008: 122) discusses a further dimension of cross-cultural theory, that of high and low context cultures: 'In low-context cultures, the message is conveyed largely by the words spoken, In high-context cultures, a good deal of the meaning is implicit, and the words convey only a small part of the message.' He identifies the USA as a low-context culture where 'verbal communication is expected to be explicit, direct, and unambiguous' and cultures like Indonesia with a style that is 'much more inexact, ambiguous, and implicit' (Thomas 2008: 122).

Different norms mean that misunderstandings can also arise from the use of silence in conversation, the use of praise, the degree of formality and the use of slang, euphemisms, idioms and proverbs.

It is not realistic to think that all leaders can be fully aware of all the implications and nuances of language and cross-cultural theories but it is worth adding reflection on these sources of confusion in communication to the 'mindfulness' and 'critical consciousness' of the individual discussed in Chapter 1.

Barriers to effective communications

Effective communication is essential for effective leadership and management. Inspection reports in England suggest that in far too many schools and colleges, communication skills are still perceived as weak: 'Communication is complex and in many schools is ineffective' (O'Sullivan et al. 1997: 108). Although communication is a complex process it is one that we take for granted and may assume that we do well. It is a fundamental part of our leadership behaviour. Jones (2005) identifies poor communication, as in our scenario of the university department, as a potential cause of conflict within organizations including teams:

> To some extent, all conflict is the product of poor communication. Team leaders need to take extra care to communicate effectively, even though it does take time. Yet, despite being time-consuming, planning how to get messages across is vital. When team members' understanding of issues is unclear they often feel insecure, and that can lead to conflict. Team members could make use of team briefings to help minimize some of the communication break-downs. Regular, but short, team briefings can help to keep the team informed of priorities, progress and policies; dispel rumours and muffle the grapevine. This free movement of information helps create a more open culture.
>
> (Jones 2005: 107)

If the head of department in our scenario had adopted a system of regular briefings plus some longer meetings to look at deeper issues affecting the department, the staff would have been much better prepared to take on the university-wide proposals constructively.

Taking time and planning frequent communication are vital to effectiveness (the same point is made about meetings in Chapter 8). Communication is about both *content* and *process*, and if what we say as leaders or managers is to be effective, it needs to be consonant with our non-verbal communication, such as eye contact and body language (see later in this chapter) and it needs to be consistent with earlier messages. Consequently, awareness of inhibiting elements, both in ourselves and others, becomes crucial if problems are to be overcome. Major communication barriers can include:

- hearing what we want to hear;
- ignoring conflicting information;
- being aware of our perceptions of the communicator;
- recognizing that words mean different things to different people; and
- acknowledging that there is often little awareness and understanding about non-verbal communication.

(Armstrong 1994: 36)

One of these barriers, being aware of our perceptions of the communicator means that it is important to recognize that we have stereotypes about leadership and about the value of types of people that prejudice our perceptions. This means that younger people, people of a minority ethnic group and women may be heard 'differently'. To take the area of gender, strong leaders of different sexes are perceived differently. For example women are notoriously seen as domineering when a man exhibiting the same style of communication might be termed decisive. In my survey of women head teachers in England it seemed that they perceived a tendency to judge women by different yardsticks from men.

> Within my LEA [local education authority], there are situations in which I have had to push for the needs of my school and am seen sometimes as difficult where a male head is seen as firm and assertive, but I can live with it! (woman secondary head, early 50s)
>
> (Coleman 2005: 28)

Although there are lots of similarities in the ways that men and women communicate, there are also many well-documented differences (Schick-Case 1994; Barrett and Davidson 2006). However, it is not just a matter of recognizing that there are differences, but of the value that is put on the difference. Barrett and Davidson (2006) state that difference can be seen as inferiority with women needing to change and adapt to male patterns of communication. They point out that:

> The management of diversity on the other hand, seeks to fully develop the potential communication skills of each employee (regardless of gender, ethnicity, disability, age and so on) and turn the different sets of skills that each employee brings into a business advantage.
>
> (Barrett and Davidson 2006: 14)

Messages are undoubtedly influenced by the motives, sex and socioculture of both parties. A parallel can be drawn between the giving and receiving of communication and the curriculum that is offered in a school or college. There you have the intended curriculum as defined by those responsible – the government, the universities, the school or college; the delivered curriculum – as mediated by the teachers and lecturers; and the received curriculum – the messages that actually get through to the students. The three: intended; delivered and received will be subtly different.

In terms of communication, Rasberry and Lemoine (1986) point to what they see as a four-stage loop moving through:

1. Intended message
2. Language encoding
3. Transmission process
4. Received (decoded) message.

Thomas (2008) points out that the intended message can be distorted at a number of stages. The communicator's skill in choosing the manner and channel of communication, for example written on paper, written email or spoken, and the skill of the receiver in decoding the message are particularly important. If the sender and the receiver have different cultural references the difficulty in ensuring that the intended message is received is compounded. Within an organization micro-political interests add to the problems of people interpreting what they hear and then passing the messages on to suit their own needs or with selective understanding. Remember the micro-political activity of the professors in the scenario at the start of this chapter.

Aiding effective communication

Effective leaders need to be effective communicators with individuals and groups – especially in articulating and transmitting their ideas and 'vision' (Beare et al. 1989). Adair's (1986) examination of how group-based communications fail suggests that in dealing with groups, clarity is vital and stresses the following:

- Having a clear understanding of what you want to say – the message objective
- Giving reasons which explain changes of practice or process
- Incrementalizing the explanation
- Relating aims to purposes and understanding the interaction.

Handy (1993) adds that managers need to take *positive* steps to overcome possible failure by, for example,

- Using more than one communication net or group
- Encouraging two-way rather then one-way communications
- Keeping as few links in the communication chain as possible.

According to Adair (1986), capable managers try to *prioritize* their communications across their organization. He suggests that they should do so according to 'three concentric circles of priority' regarding information-giving:

- What they must know
- What they should know (desirable but not essential)
- What they could know (relatively unimportant).

The interrelationships within the group may well determine the way in which messages are transmitted and translated. In a large organization it could be useful to know the ways in which information is transmitted from one individual to another. There are likely to be both formal and informal communication networks in organizations and informal networks may be linked with micro-political activity. We often refer to the informal network as the grapevine. Alternative ways of looking at networks are proposed by

Mullins (1993), who saw differing geometric patterns of communications relationships:

- *The star:* a centralized pattern with communication from the periphery to the centre and vice versa – quick answers to simple problems.
- *The chain:* centralized down to the next in the line and so on – providing multiple opportunities for misunderstanding.
- *The circle:* with people speaking to those on either side with sequential information flow but may take time to get from start to finish.
- *All channels:* a star within a circle so that messages going from periphery to centre and vice versa also travel along hierarchical chains and from person to person at the same level.

Communicating with people in groups is a vital role for leaders in education and elsewhere, but leadership also involves dealing with individuals on a one to one basis. Perhaps the most important dealings of this kind occur in the context of appraisal or performance review (see Chapter 6). The main communication skills involved in these activities are listening and giving and receiving feedback.

Communication with individuals

The major skills needing development where communication is spoken and between two individuals are the ability to listen and the ability to give feedback in situations such as observation of teaching; appraisal linked to performance management; informal or formal counselling, coaching and mentoring. Take time to reflect on the processes involved in this one to one communication. This will mean that you are really listening, planning what you are going to say and attempting to empathize with the other person in the dialogue about how your messages are received. In dialogues such as these, although listening skills and skilful and insightful feedback are vital, it is also important to be aware of the impact of body language in such relationships. Sensitivity also needs to be exercised in written communications, and the development and extensive use of email has brought about something of a revolution in the way in which we communicate with each other formally and informally at work.

Listening and hearing

Riches (1997) emphasizes the need for active listening, where the listener is actually engaged with and concentrating on what is being said. There is also a need to take into account the history of the relationship between the two individuals and of course the power relationship between them. Jones (2005: 180) gives a helpful list of things to avoid in a one to one situation, in this case coaching:

- Jumping to conclusions about what the speaker will say
- Thinking about what we are going to say next rather than listening to the speaker
- Having our mind on other things leading to a 'glazed look' at the speaker
- Blocking out what is being said because of an emotional response to it
- Trying very obviously to listen, repeating things and therefore missing new facts
- Avoiding the issue, not asking for clarification because it is all too complex
- Having your mind made up already and not allowing other ideas to challenge
- Focusing on the facts rather than what the speaker is saying about themselves
- Allowing external distractions (e.g. noise) to take over our attention.

(Jones 2005: 180)

Active listening might involve asking questions or being responsive in other ways. Work pressure might mean that managers are tempted to adopt selective or 'on-off' listening and what might be called 'false' listening (where, technically, the words are heard but the mind is not attentive). You can possibly recall incidents where you have watched the body language of someone who is supposed to be listening to you but is clearly not doing so. Hargie et al. (1994) in looking at the patterns of ways in which education managers utilize interpersonal communications, found that managers often overrated their own ability to communicate effectively and also indicate that this tendency is displayed more frequently by men than women.

> Overall, research indicates that women's communications are more other-directed, warm and mitigated than men's, and men's communications are more dominant, status-asserting, and task-oriented than women's.
>
> (Carli 2006: 76)

However, both men and women tend to be warmer in speaking to women and may be more deferential when speaking to men. Also, for some women who are in positions of power and leadership there is a tendency for them to communicate in ways that are more traditionally masculine.

> **Reflection**
>
> Among your work colleagues, who do you consider to be a good listener and why? Are you a good listener?

Giving feedback

Giving feedback on the work of an individual, for example, after classroom observation or on how a group is interacting and working together calls for a sensitive approach, and it is important to consider the effect your behaviour may have on others. Feedback can be perceived as constructive or destructive. It is constructive if it is informative and helpful. Negative feedback given skilfully with thought and advice can therefore be useful. Destructive feedback is that which leaves the recipient demoralized, angry or ashamed with nothing positive to build on and this is to be avoided if at all possible.

To ensure that feedback is constructive rather than destructive:

- Start with positive points: it is then easier for the listener to accept and deal with the negatives if good points have been acknowledged first.
- Be aware of possible cultural sensitivities such as power distance.
- Be specific: talk about specific skills and give actual examples rather than general sweeping statements.
- Where there are negatives, concentrate on things that can be changed.
- Offer alternatives and positive suggestions for change. For example, if someone in a group discussion has been ignored, suggest ways in which s/he could have been brought in to the conversation.
- Be descriptive rather than evaluative: don't make value judgements and make it clear that the views are yours. Say: 'I saw ...' or 'I heard ...' and 'In my opinion ...', rather than 'You are ...' or 'You did ...'
- Leave the other person with a choice: do not try to impose your own views.
- Consider what the feedback says about you: what you choose to comment on, and how you say it will reveal your own values, behaviour and possible prejudices. Take time to reflect on what the feedback indicates about you.

Receiving feedback

As a leader you should expect to receive feedback on your work from those you lead as well as those who lead you. There are instances where 360 degree feedback is used, and we have come across the concept of 'reverse mentoring' in Chapter 1. The following tactics should help to make the feedback as useful as possible.

- Listen to the feedback rather than immediately rejecting or arguing about it. Feedback may sometimes make you feel uncomfortable but it is important to give time for reflection and understanding. Remember the concepts of mindfulness and critical consciousness discussed in Chapter 1.
- Make sure you understand what is really being said before you respond to feedback. Check back if the meaning is not clear.
- Be aware of the perspectives of the person giving feedback including possible cultural differences.
- Check with others that the opinion is a shared one. This will often give you a more balanced view of your actions.
- Ask for feedback that would be helpful but that you are not getting.
- Decide what you will do as a result of the feedback. You should use feedback to develop your own skills. You should assess its value, and the consequences of ignoring or using it, and then make a positive decision about action or inaction.
- Feedback is not easy, but it is a valuable practice in any organization or relationship. Acknowledge the value of the process to the person who has fed back to you.

Reflection

Can you recall useful feedback that you have received? If so, how much did the points made above apply?

The importance of body language

We all transmit subliminal messages through our body language which can add to or detract from the spoken messages we are offering. This applies in large meetings, in groups and in one to one meetings. The term 'body language' seems to imply that every gesture has a particular meaning but gestures are often culturally specific and the huge variety of hand gestures and their different meanings in different cultures is so complex that 'probably the best advice is to avoid gestures until one is very sure what they mean' (Thomas 2008: 135). There are also considerable differences in the extent of eye contact that is acceptable in different cultures.

Body language is not just about gestures but includes facial expressions, the way you look at people, and your posture: 'One suggestion is that body positions that make one appear smaller indicate submissiveness and that rounded body postures communicate friendliness whereas angular postures communicate threat or hostility' (Thomas 2008: 134). Body language may also be known as non-verbal behaviour including: 'what we do with our mouths, eyebrows, eyelids and eyes, gaze, facial expressions, head movements, hands and arms and our lower limbs' (Buchanan and Huczynski 1997: 52).

Another type of non-verbal behaviour is the distance that we leave between us. That is our personal space, and what is regarded as normal differs from one culture to another. Individuals from cultures where the accepted amount of personal space is larger will feel that their space is invaded in cultures where less space is normal. The rate of speech, its pitch and its volume are also aspects of non-verbal behaviour and may indicate whether we are feeling stressed, anxious or angry although again this may be culturally defined. When undertaking research with Chinese colleagues in China (Coleman et al. 1998) we English researchers quickly gave up the idea of including observation of meetings in schools as any part of our research, as we were completely inaccurate in our judgement of the feelings of the contributors when it was based on their body language and rate, pitch and volume of speech.

In one to one meetings it is easy to transmit anxiety from one person to another through looking away, or through behaviour like playing with the hair or covering the mouth. It may be possible to monitor and change your own behaviour, but it may also be helpful to make use of a video recorder to identify and then modify traits and gestures. It is also easy to transmit positive behaviour through body language, for example a group or pair of friends may adopt 'posture mirroring' and 'gesture mirroring' when they unconsciously mimic the other's pose or action, e.g. crossing legs or putting a hand to the chin.

Knowledge of body language and the fact that it is culturally prescribed is important in communication and observation of non-verbal behaviour may give us clear indications of attitudes of others. As the person communicating, it is possible to consciously send non-verbal messages and this is potentially important in presenting ourselves to others. However, it does involve a 'level of conscious attention and control [that] may be difficult for most of us to sustain' (Buchanan and Huczynski 1997: 53).

Attentiveness and control of detail and presentation are also required in electronic communications.

Technology and communication

The implications of ICT for teaching and learning are enormous but ICT has also impacted on management, providing systems to store information and support decision-taking. In relation to communication possibly the biggest change has been the increasing use of email. However, emails written quickly and without due thought may not say what we really mean, may appear abrasive or be misinterpreted by the receiver:

> Errors are more likely to occur in communication where feedback is either absent or delayed, and where the information-rich texture of face-to-face conversation is replaced with simple written messages. The way in which we decode or perceive a brief electronic mail message may be quite different from the perception we would gain if the sender were sitting in our room and explaining the message in person.
>
> (Hoy and Miskel 2005: 63)

Messages delivered face to face are tempered by the manner of delivery including non-verbal behaviour. Emails are delivered 'straight' and the addition of an emoticon like a smiley face is an attempt (not always successful) to modify the impact of the message.

It is helpful to be aware of the possibilities of misunderstanding through the brevity of emailed messages and it is therefore a good idea to review a message before it is sent, and to delay answering an email on a sensitive matter until you have had time to think carefully about it.

Claims are made that technology and the internet are great levellers and, for example: 'inherently gender neutral' (Thomson 2006: 245). This is only likely to be the case where the gender is not known. There are indications that gender and other differentiating factors, are just as present in electronic communication as in face to face. For example, 'although polite, grammatically correct emails were in general perceived more positively, impolite emails were seen as being authored by high status males, and polite emails from competent females' (Thomson 2006: 244). In a work environment individuals may know each other and emailed communication will tend to mirror normal face to face communication so gender may impact more in emails where people do not already know each other.

It is now more common to engage in professional development through online conferencing and there are many opportunities both formal and informal to take part in such discussions. Working online in conferencing it is also important to choose words and phrases carefully to be sure that you are not misunderstood. In one study of online distance learning (ODL) the researchers identified gender concerns but also that 'the programme, the counsellors, and the motivations and personality of the learners all independently and collectively mediated the learners' (male and female) experience of ODL' (Sen and Samdup 2009: 169). Those acting as facilitators have to watch out for and deal with 'discrimination, harassment and flaming' (Thomson 2006: 246) in computer-mediated conferences where it is important to establish rules of behaviour. The concept of 'flaming' refers to the possible eruption of hostilities in the exchange of emails, where individuals have not given enough thought to the impact of their communication.

It is appropriate that the chapter ends with a focus on electronic communication as ICT offers so much potential to us now and in the future. However, as with all aspects of communication it is important that we take time to reflect and consider how best to ensure that the messages we want to transmit are accurately encoded by us, transmitted through the most appropriate medium and decoded by the receiver in a way that truly communicates our meaning.

Summary

The chapter started with consideration of the importance of communication of values of leadership on the culture and style of the organization and continued by considering the impact of national cultures and languages on communication. Barriers to communication and ways of making communication more effective were considered first as they relate to groups and then as they relate to meetings of individuals with special consideration of body, or non-verbal language. Throughout the chapter you have been urged to take time, reflect and use empathy in initiating and receiving communications of all kinds including ICT.

Further reading

The following books have a useful chapter on communication: Hoy, W.K. and Miskel, C.G. (2005) *Educational Administration: Theory, Research, and Practice*, 7th edn. Boston, MA: McGraw-Hill International Edition.

Armstrong, M. (1999) *A Handbook of Human Resource Management Practice*, 7th edn. London: Kogan Page.

For a specialist look at gender in relation to communications see: Barrett, M. and Davidson, M.J. (eds) (2006) *Gender and Communication at Work*. Aldershot: Ashgate.

4 Decision-making and the management of conflict

The taking of decisions and the manner in which they are taken are at the very heart of the leadership and management of an organization, and clearly indicate the management style adopted. Although a collegial approach is normatively seen as desirable, many organizations operate bureaucratically with little chance for individuals to participate. Alternatively, in a micro-political culture, conflict may be endemic and especially obvious around decision-taking. As well as exploring these areas, this chapter links back to the earlier chapters to discuss values and decision-making and ways of living with difference. The chapter continues with discussion of negotiation skills and assertiveness in relation to individuals and to groups.

Decision-making and leadership or management style

Decision-making and decision-taking are integral to leadership and management. Indeed in Tannenbaum and Schmidt's (1973) early model of styles of management, decision-taking is used as a proxy measure for management behaviour overall. In that model it is a question of who takes responsibility for decision-making that varies, and the extent to which staff are consulted, or told what to do, which indicate differing style of leadership and management and the values on which the organization is based. It is possible to define leadership and management styles in many ways. In practice elements of different styles exist together in an organization and its sub-units. As we saw in Chapter 3, three of the most identifiable styles are: formal (including hierarchical and bureaucratic), collegial (including transformational) and political or micro-political.

In Western cultures there has been a move away from the formal, what some call the 'heroic' (Sinclair 1999) model of leadership that is typified by 'masculine' values of decisiveness and strength toward a softer more people-centred style. Another way of putting this is that it is a change from a transactional style of leadership to a transformational one where problems are solved and improvement is achieved primarily through the development of others. In my research with secondary school head teachers in England, the dominant style claimed by the majority of both men and women was a people centred, collaborative approach. However, a move towards this style of leadership is not necessarily happening everywhere. Harber and Davies (1997) argue that in many less affluent countries, particularly those with a colonial heritage, there is a rigid and bureaucratic attitude to decision-taking which affects teachers and students:

> In terms of decision-making, bureaucracy is a rigid, closed and non-participatory form of organization, which has severe shortcomings in a contemporary world of rapid change and uncertainty.
>
> (Harber and Davies 1997: 59)

Bureaucratic organizations may have clear rules for decision-making, but the type of contextual factors present in the schools that Harber and Davies (1997) describe tend to mean that 'they do not actually operate as efficient bureaucracies anyway' but tend to be authoritarian with arbitrary decisions being made by one powerful person. They quote a study by Moll (1995) of a school where the operation of such a head is described:

> She told the other teachers what to do and to teach and when and how to do so. She set the timetable and decided on pupil admissions. . . . She spent most of her day wandering from class to class, now and then issuing curt instructions to teachers or pupils. The principal was the only person who appeared to make any decisions with regard to education matters and her style was, in regard to the formal activities of the school, extremely authoritarian.
>
> (Moll 1995: 14)

In this extreme case all decisions were made by the head teacher. In most organizations there will be a sharing of decision-taking based on the formal or informal distribution of power and authority. Rarely, decisions may be taken through consensus, but some combination of collaboration and decisiveness on the part of leaders seems to be a compromise reached in many educational organizations. According to Gold and Evans (1998) many teachers do not want to have to take part in too much decision-making. One of the disadvantages of collegiality is the time taken to come to decisions where people are expected to reach a consensus. There is also the feeling that those in positions of authority are 'paid to take decisions'. Gold and Evans (1998) consider that:

> there is a very careful balance to be found between giving too much information, asking for too much consultation from busy

people, and making uninformed decisions without any consultation. Whichever balance is found is based on the management
philosophy of the senior managers in a school, and is then made
public and clear to all the stakeholders of a school. In theory this is
an effective way to run the decision-making processes of a school.

(Gold and Evans 1998: 21)

Bringing people together to make decisions through consensus may be
seen as a collegial ideal. However, Lumby (2008) points out that trying to
come to consensus may be somewhat counter-productive in an institution
that values the diversity of its members and that rather than making an
'easy assumption of commonality' there needs to be an 'effort of understanding' (Lumby 2008: 76) in keeping with the need for reflection and
'mindfulness' on the part of leaders. Coming to a consensus not only is
time consuming and difficult but also may eliminate useful and productive differences of opinion.

In organizations where there are strong subcultures, where opposing
views are held by groups and/or individuals, micro-politics may typify the
management style. In both bureaucratic, formal styles and collegial styles
the processes of decision-making will be relatively transparent. There will
be rules or conventions concerning decision-making which mean that individuals are aware of where power is held. However, in a micro-political
management culture, decision-making will be difficult to follow or
understand as individuals and groups make 'deals' with each other within
a context of power struggles. The actions of the professors in the scenario
in Chapter 3 exemplified micro-political activity. They were using their
strength and influence to counter the more formal power of the senior
management. Gold and Evans (1998) offer a good example of how micro-
political activity can affect decision-making:

> Excessive micro-political activity may be indicative of blocked or
> ineffective decision-making routes. For example, there might be
> individual members of the management structure who do not
> fulfil their management roles, and in this case do not act as a con-
> duit for information and opinion, so other colleague work round
> them, approaching other members of staff in order to expedite or
> clarify matters.
>
> (Gold and Evans 1998: 22)

Have you become aware of close groupings of staff, of a tendency
for views to be expressed by groups rather than individuals, of increasingly difficult negotiation because the resolution of one problem becomes
linked to associated difficulties for others in the group . . . even to a sudden

cessation of conversation when you walk into a room? If so you could be experiencing micro-politics at work.

Recognizing the existence of power groups and developing management strategies to meet objections in conflict situations are important in themselves (Ball 1987), but understanding the management of the micro-politics in an organization may help even more in pre-empting conflict. Micro-political groupings often develop (or regroup) when policy matters are being discussed and when participants have a greater or lesser degree of vested interest in the outcomes (Hoyle 1986).

Hoyle (1986) has argued that leaders 'know it goes on', but frequently avoid acknowledging its existence because it is not viewed as a wholly rational or ethical process and because people feel 'unprofessional' if they get involved. For Ball (1987) micro-politics stems from different approaches to participation. He outlines adversarial, authoritarian, managerial and interpersonal approaches by leaders and the consequent reaction of the led while Hoyle (1986: 17) defines micro-politics as 'the strategies by which individuals and groups in organizational contexts seek to use their resources of authority and influence to further their interests'. He suggests that the leadership strategies used include:

- *Dividing and ruling:* so that power groups are minimized.
- *Co-opting and displacing:* so that additional forces are brought into play.
- *Controlling information:* so that groups cannot develop response strategies.
- *Controlling meetings:* so that group representatives are not allowed to dominate.

We need to recognize that there may be a gender aspect to micro-political dynamism. Women are thought to be more likely to negotiate, compromise and change allegiances according to the need of the time than are men. Kanter (1983) writing about work in industry as long ago as the early 1980s has urged that to achieve success in many micro-political environments, women need to be very careful over *how* they communicate as well as *what* they say (see Chapter 3).

In a case study focusing on micro-politics in a nursery school over a period of three years, Salo (2008) found that the micro-political perspective on decision-making was not sufficiently powerful for what took place in staff meetings. Instead, what was observed seemed more like actors in a play and he asks:

> However, what if teachers attending meetings are not at all inclined to use their power by participating in decision-making?

What if their strongest wish is to 'act' as a teacher and 'play the role of' the teacher in front of their colleagues and the Head?

(Salo 2008: 506)

This researcher rejects rational analysis, and even finds the micro-political analysis of decision-making lacking and comes to the conclusion that it can best be understood through the metaphor of 'play'.

Reflection

When you consider the most recent meeting you attended, were you able to see different power bases competing, and/or was it apparent that people were 'acting out roles'?

Decision-making and external influences

External demands may make decision-taking on the part of educational leaders more difficult. Educational policy changes in Iceland moving schools towards a more market driven approach provided a context where principals had to take decisions in difficult and contested situations (Lárusdóttir 2008) and where their values as education professionals and leaders of learning were challenged by strict target setting and monitoring:

Their [the head teachers'] narratives have drawn attention to the fact that there are times when neither knowledge nor experience are adequate, situations which have called for reflection, a search for a barometer or a criterion for something which they would usually call 'a good' solution. This has highlighted the place of values in head teachers' decision-making because it is here that the head teachers' personal and professional values and valuation processes have come into play.

(Lárusdóttir 2008: 228)

Wildy et al. (2004) have developed an instrument to investigate decision-making by school principals who they see as subject to three sets of demands, again because of policy changes. The original work on this was done in Australia and New Zealand, but the instrument has since been applied in the Netherlands and Taiwan and is to be used in other countries. According to them, principals have difficulty in embracing the following three competing demands that relate to decision-taking:

1. Accountability to education authorities, including being finally accountable for all the decisions that are made in the school.
2. Making decisions collaboratively while holding strong views themselves.
3. Making decisions collaboratively in groups even though this may not be the most efficient way of decision-making, 'wasting' the time of those involved.

The second of these competing demands was the dilemma felt by the head teacher in the scenario in Chapter 2 where she respected the views of the others on the appointment panel, but held strong views herself on who should be appointed. In that situation more discussion about values might have helped the situation.

In a higher education context, Williams (2009) identifies some of the leadership dilemmas that deans of business schools have to handle. They include decisions about structures (e.g. departmental versus a faculty structure), pedagogy (e.g. face to face or distance learning and teaching) and culture (e.g. maximizing student numbers versus the quality of students entering the business school):

> Underlying these dilemmas are clashes between old and new cultures, that is academic values relating to autonomy and knowledge generation and management values relating to competitiveness and financial control.
>
> (Williams 2009: 135)

It is pointed out that there are no right or wrong decisions to make as each choice could benefit aspects of the business school. In practice it was up to the deans 'to give a lead by initiating and/or supporting appropriate change, given the mission and objectives of the school' (Williams 2009: 136).

In these cases it may be underlying values that determine how decisions are made.

Values in decision-making

Values may be especially apparent in decision-making in difficult situations. In an example focusing on Quebec Province School Superintendents (Langlois 2004: 82–84) researchers identified stages of decision-making in really difficult situations. Some of those identified were: instances of fraud in their organizations; having to fire school principals; allegations of sexual harassment towards students; demoting employees and dealing with grievances as a result of dismissals or demotions.

Research showed that the superintendents tended to take a problem-solving approach, which went through eight overlapping and successive stages. These were:

1. Responding to and acting upon a given situation. When they were aware of the urgency of the matter they took responsibility and tended to 'take things immediately in hand'.
2. Checking the rules, standards and school district policies. This involved checking whether there were legal issues to take into account or procedures that they should follow.
3. Becoming ethically aware of the dilemma. At this stage they focus on the fact that there is no one right course of action and they fall back on the 'values, principles and responsibilities' upon which they will base their decision. They are also likely to consult a trusted colleague or friend at this stage.
4. The ethical analysis stage. This is a type of a review of the situation so far, which is where they bring in personal and professional values. The analysis of this crucial stage ends with a decisive element which 'consists of recognizing which values are non-negotiable'.
5. Despite this non-negotiability, they will seek support for their decision from those to whom they are accountable and then prepare to present it to those concerned.
6. A meeting with those concerned takes place when the decision-maker announces the decision 'frankly, but always with consideration for others'.
7. Concluding the decision-making process. This might involve writing a report.
8. Assessing the consequences and effects on the organization. Closure of the problem, although there may be further rounds and repercussions, for example if one of the parties has a grievance.

Overall, it seemed essential that the superintendents were able to stand back from the situation, assess the consequences of their decision and be confident about explaining their decision, when called on to do so. They felt it was essential for them to be consistent and have moral responsibility.

Reflection

If you have been faced with decision-making in a difficult and sensitive situation were those the stages that you went through?

The need for educational leaders to make decisions has been examined by Robbins and Trabichet (2009) in the light of living in a multicultural society. They propose that educational leadership training programmes should include consideration of ethics. They conclude that educational leaders in multicultural societies seeking resolution of dilemmas 'must look at their own place in relation to these cultures and thus understand any cultural bias he or she many have' (Robbins and Trabichet 2009: 55). These sentiments are very much in keeping with the predominant values of this book.

Managing conflict: Living with difference

You will have realized that unless there is complete stability within an organization, there will always be the potential for discussion, some difference of opinion, downright disagreement or pernicious disharmony. In this section we will be looking at the notion of conflict. However, you are urged to move from the view that conflict is necessarily a negative and destructive force to recognize its potential for growth and development although it presents a challenging situation to leaders. The following scenario illustrates conflict and its management.

Scenario: Conflict over change in a South African school

As part of some research into leadership in South African schools, a township school reported on the management of decision-making. Although the findings have contributed to other research, part of the evidence helps us to understand how conflict develops. Contextually this secondary school has 1,300 students up to age 16 with 40 staff and has been under considerable pressure to enhance external examination results despite the three problems of inadequate staffing (the ratio is 1 teacher for 40 pupils), inadequate building and equipment, with particular pressure on rooms to allow for work with those following science and technology, and staffing problems arising from difficulty in recruitment into a socio-culturally difficult area.

As part of the national policy, Curriculum 2005, there are many ongoing changes in the organization and delivery of the curriculum. These are summed up by the Southern African Historical Society in 2006 in the following statement:

> We welcome the break with the old authoritarian and rote learning styles of the past. We welcome also its commitment to equality in teaching and training; its recognition of the urgent need

to create more and better opportunities for entrance to and from all levels of teaching and training; its greater recognition of skills and qualifications obtained in job-related training; its identification of the need to promote lifelong learning; its promotion of a more direct integration of learning and training, of knowledge and skills to educate and train people who can do things; its more rational integration of knowledge and skills in different learning areas, emphasising co-operative learning and the development of a basic understanding of what is learned and why it is learned; its recognition of the importance of an outcomes-based approach to teaching and training; and its promotion of critical thinking and civic responsibility.

(Southern African Historical Society 2006)

For the staff of the school, however, there are many problems. They have grown up with authoritarian approaches and rote learning and continue to see this as the only means of coping with educating large classes with limited equipment and resources. They belong to a highly unionized profession that is only slowly moving to accept changes in approach and have been working to secure some sort of trade-off in enhanced preparation time, additional staffing resources and salary payments in recognition of the additional demands for training, teaching and behaviour management. Additionally, the low rate of staff turnover and the hierarchical awareness of long-serving staff have led to entrenched opposition to change. This has been exacerbated because of the appointment of a coloured woman principal working with a predominately African staff.

Her management of curriculum change shows how conflict can be defused. After her appointment she made a statement that all staff would be equally valued and the opinion of everyone would be considered in the management of change. This was not well received by the senior management team of two deputy principals and three associate principals. Their view was that the school had always suffered when change upset established routines and when members of staff felt that they were being asked to express views which were then ignored. One of the associate principals (the most recent appointment, and the only one to have undertaken a postgraduate leadership course) argued that there was a case for working with, rather than against, the principal and that it might be helpful to seek her views of the long-term vision for the school.

The concept of vision seemed inappropriate to the remainder of the group but they were convinced that 'while the principal is looking at vision she won't be interfering in the classroom' and so it was agreed that they would work with her. At this stage the principal was asked by her governing body to outline her strategy for the development of the school.

Her response was that it was important for everyone to be involved and she established a series of professional development meetings at which the question was 'What sort of a school do you want to work in?' She asked that each working group (curriculum subject staff, pastoral and behaviour staff, activities staff and the senior management team) should respond with one short paragraph at the end of the meeting.

The groups duly met and then realized how complex a simple question was. Joe, a senior science teacher, spoke at the curriculum group and argued for the retention of a very tight discipline hold so that 'we know where we stand' but he also realized that the most able students needed the opportunity of experiential learning which had a greater freedom to it. Arusha, subject leader for the humanities group of subjects, argued for a more relaxed approach to discipline so that 'the students can become responsible citizens within the school community'. Walter, subject leader for mathematics and computer skills, and a strong union representative, argued that you could not achieve any progress without more resources and so the school would have to continue as it was. After two hours of diametrically opposed views, the group moved to secure some unanimity. At this point one of the younger staff, Angel, said: 'I have listened to you all and said little but I am aware of the fact that we all want the best for our students despite the problems you have outlined, and so I propose that we set out our ideal and then outline the most important problems to be overcome.' This led to the curriculum group report being stated in the following way:

> We feel that we should be moving to a curriculum that is broad, challenging and interesting but we will not be able to attain it without enhanced resources and more staff training.

While this was indicative of progress, Walter went back to the staff room and gathered a group of older staff around him to argue that whatever the ownership of change it would mean more work and that individualized learning was a 'noble aim but unattainable and so the principal should be told that she needed to be part of the real world'. This antagonism bubbled on for some weeks and the principal became aware of staff unrest. After some discussion with the chairperson of the school governing body, she decided to meet the opposition from what she saw as an influential group of people.

To do so she asked Walter to join the vision planning committee whose task was to ascertain the vision for the school, in the light of the statements from all the staff groups. She told a daily staff meeting that no vision could be achieved without cost, but that, as part of the work, she would ask the planning committee to identify practices that were taking precious time so that there would be no implementation of vision without a compensating gain from unnecessary procedures, and she had a special meeting of the governing body at which she outlined her three priorities for the coming year.

These were

- To secure improved behaviour with recourse to positive rather than negative discipline
- To seek financial support from the community associations so that everybody had a stake in the improved school
- To develop a staff development programme meeting the needs of each individual so that, when agreed, they would all be able to work for the new vision.

The story goes on but the principal gained by marginalizing and then involving the opposition, giving time as well as seeking changed practice and maintaining a strong stand as the leader for a changed school.

We have already looked at the importance of communication in Chapter 3, and if we think of the resolution of conflict as the opportunity to re-establish communication then the organization, and more importantly, human relationships do not suffer. Handy (1993: 108) uses the basic concept of 'difference' in identifying the nature of conflict and, using a pluralist perspective, he distinguishes between three kinds of difference:

- that arising from 'argument'
- that arising from 'competition' between participants
- that which reflects genuine 'conflict' arising from some deep-seated cause.

He then suggests four strategies for working through difference:

- shared leadership, offering open discussion
- confidence and trust in others, letting them express their views
- challenging tasks, involving interpersonal activity
- making full use of group member resources.

These differences and strategies can be seen in the scenario above, where the new principal followed all four steps. The strategies can be seen more generally working across education – for example in planning for subject progression in primary and secondary schools or in curriculum meetings planning new subject combinations in further and higher education – although where people seek to enhance self- or peer-esteem or wish to gain senior management support, competition may become apparent. Handy (1993) notes that at the productive or 'fruitful' level, some degree of competition may be helpful, first, in setting standards, second, in stimulating and channelling energies, and third, in 'sorting things out' – distinguishing better from worse.

> **Reflection**
>
> Think of one of the examples of conflict within your organization. Are they more than merely 'difference' and to what extent could the Handy strategies have been of value in resolving problems?

Where Handy (1993: 108) sees conflict as 'harmful difference', it is characterized by:

- poor communication, both laterally and vertically
- inter-group hostility and jealousy
- interpersonal friction
- escalation to arbitration
- proliferation of rules, regulations, norms and myths
- low morale over apparent inefficiency.

This situation may arise to a greater or lesser extent during any decision-making process. Handy (1993) argues that two basic management strategies are available to deal with conflict:

- *Control by ecology strategy* (often seen as fruitful competition), which harnesses the cultural forces within an organization.
- *Regulations strategy*, which uses formalized control through mechanistic approaches and control of power to listen and then impose change.

The former way of resolution (adopted by the principal in the scenario) may be time-consuming and rely heavily on the values structure of the organization but it is less negative than the latter which imposes a will on the basis of power. The former way also ensures that the organization benefits from the range of diversity of its members.

Armstrong (1994) advises that those who wish to resolve conflict need to:

- listen actively
- observe as well as listen
- help people to understand and define the problem
- allow feelings to be expressed
- encourage alternative solutions
- get people to develop their own implementation plans.

This type of conflict resolution can be seen in the scenario, where the overall approach might be seen as 'collaborative' (Armstrong 1999: 656). This is one approach and was appropriate because the conflict was about important matters. However, the conflict may not always be about important things. Armstrong (1999) identifies other approaches to conflict resolution in different circumstances. These include:

- *Avoiding:* where an issue is trivial
- *Compromising:* to reach a quick agreement
- *Accommodating:* not upsetting the other person when you are wrong.

Although there may be different levels and types of conflict, it is worth remembering the following generalizations from research on teacher participation in decision-making. The findings generally indicate the following:

- The opportunity to share in formulating policies is important for morale.
- It is positively related to the teachers' satisfaction with the profession.
- Teachers prefer principals who involve them in decision-making.
- Decisions fail because they are not accepted by subordinates.
- Teachers neither expect nor want to be involved in every decision.
                                                     (Hoy and Miskel 2005: 323)

Difficult individuals

Schacter (1951) has indicated that where a member of a close-knit team disagrees significantly or displays apparently 'deviant' behaviours – whether in team-meetings or elsewhere – communication with the individual is, at least initially, likely to increase dramatically in order to 'problem solve' and 'bring the person round'. Where the 'deviant' behaviour persists, communication efforts are likely to peak, the group 'cuts its losses', and communications rapidly decline, with individuals sometimes being told openly of their 'rejection'. On a more positive note, Belbin (1993: 67) recommends that where there is a 'difficult' person in a team, efforts should be made to 'seek positive leads from what may seem an unwelcome trait'. For example, he suggests that someone who is cynical may have the ability to analyse and make judgements and that this ability which has 'gone sour' may be harnessed to more positive ends by asking for an opinion on a relatively neutral matter and so engaging them with the work of the team.

In our scenario, Walter shows some aspects of being a difficult individual, although his role as union representative means that he has to challenge changes that might impact negatively on staff. The new principal engages him in an important committee who are charged with finding ways of cutting the work of staff to compensate for any change that brings more work.

Gold and Evans (1998) suggest that working with a particular individual who is 'difficult' may be addressed by the following tactics:

- Acknowledging the uncomfortable feelings aroused in you by your difficult person, then trying to put the feelings aside to work objectively with the problem.
- Separating the person from the problem.
- Taking time to think about your next action.
- Developing a network of people so that you can support each other.
- Planning your actions carefully, discussing them with others or at least rehearsing the conversation with yourself.

(adapted from Gold and Evans 1998: 44–45)

Negotiation skills

Negotiation skills have become increasingly important in the context of a more marketized education service because so many resource issues have to be locally managed. Lowe and Pollard (1989: 187) suggest that 'frame of mind' is as important as what is said. They see the twin tensions of push and pull, otherwise understood as win or lose, in competition, and argue that successful negotiation often stems from the ability for both sides to think that they have gained in some way – seen as a win-win situation in which both can claim to have gained.

- Common goals exist: clear and shared organizational/group purposes.
- There is openness about how to progress towards clear goals.
- Failure is not punished but is seen as productive learning.

There are differing estimates of the number of stages of the negotiation process, but the Graham (1987) four-stage model identified in Thomas (2008: 138) proposes that business negotiations follow the following stages:

1. Non-task sounding or relationship building.
2. Task-related exchange of information.
3. Persuasion.
4. Making concessions and reaching agreement.

Although these stages seem universal, the 'content duration and importance of each of these stages can be seen to differ across cultures' (Thomas 2008: 138), with more time being taken on the first two stages in Japan and China and less in the USA.

Similarly the style of negotiation may vary, with three identified styles: rational, the appeal to logic; affective where the appeal is to the emotions and finally the ideological. Culturally there is also a difference in the preference for confrontation or for more restrained and subtle bargaining. Reference to the Hofstede (1991) dimensions (see Introduction) may be helpful in predicting how cultures may differ.

Reflection

Think back to the scenario earlier in the chapter. How would you have gone about negotiating the curriculum change with one of the teachers entrenched against change.

Assertiveness

Assertiveness is an important part of negotiation and should be differentiated from aggressiveness. Back and Back (1990: 1–2) see assertive behaviour in:

- Standing up for your own rights in such a way that you do not violate another person's rights.
- Expressing your needs, wants, opinions, feelings and beliefs in direct, honest and appropriate ways.

While aggressive behaviour involves:

- Standing up for your own rights, but doing so in such a way that you violate the rights of other people.
- Ignoring or dismissing the needs, wants, opinions, feelings or beliefs of others.
- Expressing your own needs, wants and opinions (which may be honest or dishonest) in inappropriate ways.

Assertiveness is preferable to aggressiveness in negotiation, but there are also passive and manipulative ways of operating.

When you want to express your ideas, opinions, needs and feelings, you have four basic choices:

- To respond aggressively and either face the hostility of the other person, or know you have put that person down, for example through sarcasm or by being patronizing.
- To respond non-assertively (passively), putting yourself down or withdrawing from the situation, this approach can indicate a lack of self-esteem.
- To respond manipulatively, throwing out hints and hoping that the other person gets the point; the danger with this is that the other person may be resentful if they feel they are being manipulated.
- To respond assertively, making your statement in a calm, confident and direct way, always keeping in sight the needs of the other person.

Assertion is the direct and honest expression of feelings, needs and opinions. It enables you to stand up for yourself without losing compassion or sensitivity, and with a genuine respect for the other person. Assertive behaviour is associated with self-knowledge, self-respect and respect for others.

Assertive behaviour means taking control of your own life, neither blaming others, nor believing that others are responsible for your choices or behaviour. It allows you to express feelings openly and effectively without fearing ridicule, rejection or guilt, and to set limits so that others know where they stand with you.

Group conflict

While it is possible to see our activities in terms of individual behaviours, there is a collective element, and when conflict affects inter-group relationships regulatory strategies are often used. According to Handy (1993: 311–312), these include the following:

- *Arbitration:* particularly helpful for highly specific issues.
- *Rules and procedures:* although part of 'bargaining', can constrain and inhibit permanent solutions.
- *Coordinating devices:* 'boxing the problem' by marginalizing people into 'new' roles.
- *Confrontation:* being 'upfront' and challenging.
- *Separation:* providing a 'cooling off period'.
- *Neglect:* ignoring issues which seem trivial or irresolvable, but can stifle productive work.

Everard et al. (2004) consider how far conflict is avoidable. They suggest that if it moves from being individually focused to group-based, attitudes can harden and 'win-lose' situations prevail. Creating 'win-win' solutions can be difficult, however, because personal attitudes are often the hardest management 'nuts' to crack. In addition, options for resolution may be constrained by the professional context, organizational ethos and, ultimately, even the framework of employment rights. Resort to law can sometimes inhibit 'common sense' solutions. Armstrong (1994) highlights the following as the four negotiation stages:

- *Preparing:* setting objectives, obtaining information and determining strategy.
- *Opening:* revealing your bargaining position.
- *Bargaining:* spotting weaknesses in the other person's case and convincing them of the need to 'move'.
- *Closing:* recognizing the impossibility of further compromise.

Everard et al. (2004) offer a similar framework, but one built on achieving goals rather than resolving win-win, win-lose, lose-lose types of conflict. This process begins by assuming that agreement will be reached and Mulholland (1991) suggests that both parties should compare and contrast their options, judge and evaluate the ideas, clarify and test the views expressed, and then establish and reiterate goals as the criteria for successful closure. This requires an established discipline of procedure that all parties are prepared to follow.

The ability to negotiate and settle issues reveals much about how communication skills are used, the communications environment and process, and how far progress is achieved without either party losing face. Such skills are fundamental in developing good relationships both at individual and team levels.

Reflection

Think of an issue within your organization where group negotiation has been necessary. Did the resolution show 'good practice'?

Summary

This chapter has considered the vital area of decision-making, and the links with styles of leadership and management and underlying values. Particular attention was given to micro-politics and its relationship to conflict with some examples of how conflict may be managed. The chapter finished by considering the skills of negotiation and the importance of assertiveness.

Further reading

For a chapter on general and theoretical business approach to conflict and decision-taking, see: Hoy, W.K. and Miskel, C.G. (2005) *Educational Administration: Theory, Research, and Practice,* 7th edn. Boston, MA: McGraw-Hill International.

For a more detailed discussion of micro-politics see the following, which looks at the theoretical basis of micropolitics and then at research into its impact and management through differing leadership styles: Blase, J. and Anderson, G. (1999) *The Micropolitics of Educational Leadership: From Control to Empowerment.* New York: Teachers College Press.

And then, affecting whole school policy, see: Lindle, J.C. (1999) What can the study of micropolitics contribute to the practice of reforming schools? *School Leadership and Management* 19(2): 171–178.

5 Motivation and delegation

In this chapter we are concerned with the way in which people might balance their motivation as individuals with their shared efforts and contributions to their organization. However individuals perform, they are also members of teams and groups, and the organization as a whole offers an environment encouraging, or sometimes, discouraging to their effort. There is a relationship between the individual and the organization and vice versa; this relationship leads us from considering motivation to thinking about the distribution of responsibilities within the team or organization through the process of delegation. This can bring tensions especially within a professional environment and the way in which these are managed, and by implication, the organization is led, has an impact on personal satisfaction, organizational culture and organizational success. In this chapter we look at the way in which motivation can inspire individuals, using an example from our research into diversity issues. We then look at the ways in which delegation can open up opportunities for individuals and the organization.

Scenario: Interview on career progress

Gerry was interviewed about his career progress so far. He is of Caribbean descent and had grown up in South London, emerging as a star student at a local comprehensive school. He is now a lecturer at a rural college of further education in the UK and has been in his present post ever since leaving university five years ago. He had completed the postgraduate teacher training course in social sciences and embarked enthusiastically on his career. Gerry is a member of a four staff subject group within a much larger humanities faculty of thirty staff.

He reported that early in his time at the college he realized that he was not fully enjoying his work but because of family ties he thought that he would have to stay in the area and hoped that 'things might get better'. He had a college mentor during his first two years but the support had been somewhat limited and although he had been observed teaching on three occasions, there had been very limited feedback. 'To be doing all right' was not a sufficient commendation for him and he went back to talk with his former college tutor.

She probed the sources of Gerry's unhappiness. In part it was a reflection of the teaching load which was made up of 70 per cent provision of personal and social education (PSE) courses for students taking a range of two-year vocational courses, and the other 30 per cent contribution to academic A and AS economics courses. The PSE courses he described as 'hard work because the students don't really want to be with me and they would be far happier in their vocational courses', and teaching the economics was 'not really satisfying because he was being told exactly what to teach by the head of subject'. There were two other main problems, however. Gerry saw himself as 'being a sole male in a subject area dominated by able women' and 'socially at a disadvantage because of the very few people of minority ethnic background locally'. After further discussion the ex-tutor suggested that Gerry should seek an interview with the head of department and set out why he felt so unhappy.

The head of department, John, who Gerry described as 'old enough to be my grandfather', asked Gerry to prepare for their meeting and assured him that anything he wanted to say would be treated in confidence although there would have to be a formal agreed minuting of the meeting. When Gerry began to set down his concerns, he realized that he was still a junior member of staff and that he had not shared his feelings during development with any other member of staff, or indeed, with anyone in the local community. He went to his meeting and began by saying that he recognized his own problems but that he felt that he could be doing so much more for the college. And that was to prove the key to a successful outcome . . . as we shall see later in this chapter.

Motivation of ourselves and others

Whatever the nature of the team and the interrelationships between colleagues, successful education depends upon motivation at all levels – as leaders, as followers and as learners. Much has been written about motivation stemming from stimulating workers within the industrial context to maximize output. Such a mechanistic view is not strictly applicable within education and there is much concern about the inapplicability of differing forms of payment by results (however it is disguised) to human interaction, particularly in education. For most educationalists the more humanistic approach of encouragement, self-development and professionalism are more appropriate, and performance management can ensure that educational teams are supported in securing effective schools and colleges.

Several authors, who based their work on research into the functioning of mainly white upper-working-class or middle-class males in industrial settings, have added much to our understanding of the way in which people can be motivated. As always, critical evaluation prompts us to ask whether the results would have been different if the gender, class or cultural composition of participants had been different. Maslow (1943) established a hierarchy of needs and saw motivation as the spur for our progression. These are:

- *Physiological needs* (the lowest level), i.e. 'homeostasis' (the body's automatic efforts to function normally) and covers the need for food, water, sleep, sex.
- *Safety and security needs,* i.e. the need for security, freedom from pain, physical attack, predictability, orderliness.
- *Social needs,* i.e. the need for affection, a sense of belonging, social activities, friendship and for giving or receiving love.
- *Self-esteem or ego needs,* i.e. the need for self-respect, confidence, personal reputation, and esteeming others.
- *Self-actualization needs* (the highest level), i.e. involves realizing one's full potential – what Maslow describes as 'becoming everything that one is capable of becoming'.

There is considerable discussion of the nature of self-actualization. Boeree (1999) summarizing the characteristics of the individuals selected by Maslow as examples of people reaching this level points out that:

> they enjoyed solitude, and were comfortable being alone. And they enjoyed deeper personal relations with a few close friends and family members, rather than more shallow relationships with many people. They enjoyed autonomy, a relative independence from physical and social needs. And they resisted enculturation, that is, they were not susceptible to social pressure to be 'well adjusted' or to 'fit in' – they were, in fact, nonconformists in the best sense. They had an unhostile sense of humour – preferring to joke at their own expense, or at the human condition, and never directing their humour at others.
>
> (Boeree 1999: 7)

These seem to be very exceptional people, but with one exception were all male. The assumption was that they represented the norm. This raises issues about the way in which males and females progress to, and experience, self-actualization, and it may well be that reconsideration of Maslow's evidence in the light of current understanding of gender could lead to different conclusions. Is it likely that more women than men show the leadership characteristics outlined above? If so it would be expected that a higher proportion than actually evident should progress to senior leadership positions. Research (e.g. Davidson 1997; Powney et al. 2003; Coleman 2005) shows that this is not so.

McGregor (1960) also did not consider variables such as gender. He argued that motivation is dependent upon the attitudes of participants. He suggested that there are two sets of contrasting assumptions about people and work – Theory X and Theory Y.

According to McGregor (1960), Theory X assumes that most people

- inherently dislike work and are lazy
- are self-centred and lack ambition: indifferent to their organization's needs they have to be coerced, directed, controlled or threatened in order to achieve at work
- prefer to be directed, wish to avoid responsibility and, above all, want security.

By contrast, Theory Y assumes that most people

- are, by nature, physically and mentally energetic: work is as natural to them as rest and play; laziness results from poor experiences at work
- do not need to be externally controlled or directed: people can exercise internal self-control and self-direction when working towards objectives to which they are personally committed
- will seek and accept responsibilities under the right conditions
- have the capacity to exercise a high degree of creativity, imagination and ingenuity and become passive and resistant to the organization's needs only because of the way they have been treated.

Following research in industrial contexts, Herzberg (1966) suggested that as we consider our actions, we are driven by maintenance factors (he called them 'hygienes') and motivational factors (he called these 'satisfiers'). 'Hygienes' may be taken for granted as when new crockery is provided for the staff room because people think it should be there anyway as a right, but 'satisfiers' do prompt some further effort for example when teachers recognize that they are being effectively involved in policy development. Hean and Garrett (2001) considered the different causes of satisfaction and dissatisfaction in secondary science teaching in Chile but their findings can be re-echoed throughout the world. Sources of satisfaction included interactions with students, relationships within the school, and opportunities to contribute to the future development of society. Against these aspirational gains, dissatisfaction was related to poor salary, excessive workload, student characteristics, and problems with resources and infrastructure (hygienes). Thomas (2008) considers how cross-cultural issues affect motivation. He points to the way in which cultural background affects the skill variety offered by people; the way in which they perceive the task identity for a particular role and the importance or 'task significance' attaching to that role. Cultural issues may also affect autonomy in working and feedback in performance especially where the leadership style may be inherently male dominated and authoritarian.

> ## Reflection
>
> Consider your own work situation and list the factors that motivate, and those that are demotivating. How are they recognized and acted upon by the leadership to whom you are responsible?

It is generally accepted that much human behaviour is driven towards achieving goals in order to satisfy particular needs. Reflecting on the motivation literature Handy and Aitken (1986) divide motivation theories into three categories:

- *Need theories:* these maintain that an individual acts in order to meet a need or set of needs; for the teacher this may be seen as working so that there is some chance of meeting the basic needs for food, shelter and warmth and then moving on to enjoy a better life.
- *Goal theories:* these argue that we direct our actions in order to achieve particular goals. These may not be the means to an end but simply the achievement of something for its own sake; for the educationalist. This may be through reaching a particular competence level or recognizing capacity to cope with particular standards by students or encouraging creative activity.
- *Self theories:* these hold that we act to maintain or improve our image of ourselves and therefore our sense of self-respect. This may reinforce our beliefs in what is good in ourselves, what is good in the organization of which we are part, and what we hope to achieve in the future.

Handy (1993) points out that elements of all three types of motivation theory may be evident in a person, and that they may vary over time. He offers a list of assumptions, the understanding of which may help leaders to recognize and respond to varying organizational problems.

- *Rational-economic assumption:* people can be driven to complete tasks because they know that they need to achieve their economic needs as seen in pursuing further training and development.
- *Social assumption:* people gain their sense of identity through relationships with other people and that the effective leader can mobilize and use these social relationships – hence the growing

importance of team development in aspects of school and college management.

- *Self-actualizing assumption:* people are primarily self-motivated and self-controlled, making them able to integrate their own goals with those of the organization if given the opportunity – the basic thinking behind rewards systems.
- *Complex assumption:* at any one time many motives will be at work but they may not all need to be satisfied at the same time since much depends on a personal assessment of the appropriateness of the situation for need satisfaction.
- *Psychological assumption:* that people are complex and maturing organisms, passing through psychological and physiological stages of development. People evolve an 'ego ideal' towards which they strive: over and above their basic drives, the importance of self-esteem in behaviour management.

Reflection

How would you apply Handy's classification of theories to the culture of motivation within a school or college known to you? Do different people accord with different theories?

Theory into practice

Concentration on individual characteristics leads to the 'humanistic' view of motivation in education as shown by Moss (1999) who has considered the view of American researchers who commend the ideal of the 'transcendental teacher'. This is one who overcomes all the contextual and organizational inhibitors to teach in an energetic and enriching manner with 'calm presence and a sense of humour'. He argues that skilled leadership can promote cultural and attitudinal changes in the classroom helping teachers to aspire to the ideal, but does not underestimate the effort involved. Canter and Canter (2001) argue that for this approach to be successful leaders need to do the following:

- *Define the mission:* the principles that underpin the purpose and practice of teaching.
- *Turn round negative assumptions:* rephrasing the negative in a way that fits the mission.

- *Reframe problems:* going beyond the negative statement to find the real problem.
- *Build trust:* minimizing stress and welcoming contact reduces the possibility of misunderstanding.

Such an approach focuses on the link between the teacher and the work of the school or college, the link between the mission and the pedagogy of the classroom and the link between teacher and learner, and between teachers. If this can be achieved there is then motivation for leaders to lead effectively, and for the led to feel that they are driven forward by positive corporate and individual achievement. In this situation there is no view of 'carrot and stick' motivation, but rather that all concerned are driven forward by the wish to achieve.

The wish to achieve is fundamental to educational improvement and relies on the way in which people interact. The importance of the management of relationships at school and departmental or phase level has been identified by Hay McBer (2000) as fundamental to the development of 'classroom climate' in their model of teacher effectiveness. Climate can be summed up as 'a measure of the collective perceptions of pupils regarding those dimensions of the classroom environment that have a direct impact on their capacity and motivation to learn' (Hay McBer 2000: 1.1.5).

Enhancing the motivation to learn is surely the fundamental goal of education and the relationship between leadership team and teachers, and between teacher and taught is variously one of inspiring, cajoling or coercing participants to undertake a programme of work in a way that will enhance learning and achievement.

Importantly, in the context of education and teaching, the bigger the difference between the 'ego ideal' of the teacher and his or her self-perception, the more they become angry with themselves and the more they feel guilty, when they cannot attain their objectives. Because work is part of our identity (i.e. our ego ideal), it is important that opportunities are provided for all colleagues to work towards their perceived ideal and thus become motivated. The assumptions we have about the way in which people are motivated will obviously lead us to adopt different approaches to motivating people in organizations. Thus, an assumption that humans are 'rational-economic' leads to a bargaining approach and to a concern with the benefits that education will bring. The adoption of 'self-actualizing' or 'psychological' assumptions is likely to show itself in a greater concern with creating development opportunities in teaching and learning.

Handy's (1993) model, described as the motivation calculus, extends Maslow (1943) as he suggests that our motivation is driven by a more complex set of circumstances than 'needs' alone. These include our own interpretations and assessments of our working context which then form additional layers or filters in determining our response. Handy (1993) shows how individuals focus on the way that the individual deals with individual decisions, and he outlines the notion of the 'psychological contract' that each individual develops with the group that he or she becomes involved with. He categorizes organizations according to the type of psychological contract which predominates and points out that the contract is usually 'calculative'. It can, however, be cooperative or, where the contract is not freely entered into, coercive. The cultural norms of the organization can affect the way in which this contract is worked out in reality.

Evans (2003) in a comparative study of school teacher morale and that of teachers in higher education in England found that in schools: 'those who reported low levels of job satisfaction and, in some cases motivation, attributed their negative attitudes to poor leadership and management in their schools' (Evans 2003: 143). The academics in higher education were not influenced by departmental leadership but they were affected by institutional leadership because it affected the ethos of their working context. She claims that it is not leadership itself that is the factor that influences attitudes but 'it is the medium through which are transmitted the values and ideologies represented by the contexts in which people work' (Evans 2003: 143).

Values and ideologies can underpin institutional attitudes to 'outsiders' (see Chapter 1). Powney et al. (2003), drawing on a survey of 2158 teachers in England, found that teachers from black and multiethnic backgrounds enter the profession later, and have lower satisfaction levels. Powney et al. (2003) suggest that late entry is one of several organizational and personal factors affecting participation in leadership roles (52 per cent of BME staff in schools remain classroom teachers compared with 29 per cent of white women and 35 per cent of white males). Motivation is likely to play a part as there is evidence of hidden discrimination within social and institutional cultures for teachers securing promotion. The authors identified barriers including marginalization, indirect racist attitudes and post-ghettoization – all compounded by a glass ceiling which is particularly serious for women. Harris et al. (2003), in a literature review of the career progress of deputy heads, note reliance on informal networks and school or college encouragement from which ethnic minorities are often excluded. The cultural environment of teachers is also of significance – women and Muslims, for example, can be unintentionally alienated and excluded from networks by the male-dominated, Friday evening post-cricket-match pub visit at the end of the week. These issues must be addressed if motivation is to be facilitated and the highest potential levels of satisfaction are to be available to all.

Scenario: Interview on career progress (continued)

And that brings us back to Gerry. He went to talk to John and their meeting followed the agenda set by Gerry which was: my job; my future and myself. It was agreed that the work programme being followed by Gerry was not the most stimulating but that it was unlikely that there could be much change given the current pattern of recruitment by the college. John recognized the situation and said: 'The problem is that you want to get up the Maslow ladder and we can't help you much.' When they talked about the future, Gerry said that he was anxious to get wider experience but John said that that might have to come from a change of job.

Gerry was usually reluctant to talk about himself but did so on this occasion, 'and it was then that the grandfather in John came out'. He pointed out that Gerry was rather self-centred and that he had let opportunities locally pass him by – discounted squash club membership, the need for a social secretary for the staff common room and a request for a member of staff to become a school governor had all come Gerry's way but been rejected. John asked Gerry to think about their talk and to let him have a plan of action that could be shared with the head of subject.

After the shock of John's reminders Gerry realized that 'rather than being done to, I had to do something myself'. His plan was to develop some new approaches to teaching personal and social education 'as my own speciality', with a request for training time to do so, to ask for reconsideration of the rejected opportunity to serve as a governor when another opportunity occurred, and to be more determined to share his ethnic music interests with a student group. All these plans could be related to the classical motivation theorists but in John's terms were a 'splendid example of self-actualization'. Further motivation occurred when the head of subject asked Gerry to take full responsibility for AS Economics course organization. Gerry's comment, reflecting on John's ability to plant ideas in other people's minds, was: 'I wonder where that has come from?' The success of delegation is another story!

(based on interviews for Glover 2006)

Delegation

One of the most significant ways in which colleagues can be given self-ideal is through delegation of responsibility. Self-actualization may well be promoted by the enhanced self-esteem that comes with a changed role, and with the understanding that others have of this. Hierarchic responsibility structures create the environment within which others perceive downward delegation to operate – strengthened by line-management structures. Collegial structures, however, encourage distributed leadership, meaning that individuals undertake responsibility for aspects of organization, but with a greater emphasis on shared responsibility. There may be a link between gender and perceptions of leadership, for example Fletcher and Kaeufer (2003) found that female leaders are more willing to encourage others to share in strategic development. However, Coleman (2002: 119) found that most men and women head teachers saw themselves as 'collaborative and people orientated'. In a major study of the research literature on the use of distributed leadership within schools PricewaterhouseCooper (2007) note that:

> Perhaps one of the strongest themes to emerge from this existing literature on effective school leadership (as well, incidentally, as studies on leadership in the private sector), relates to the importance of developing staff, nurturing talent and, related to this, 'distributing' leadership throughout the organization. Within the schools context, distributing leadership is a potential means of ameliorating some of the workload issues which are currently being faced by school leaders, by making the role more attractive and the size of the job more deliverable. But distributed leadership is about much more than just sharing out tasks. Rather, it also encompasses a shared approach to strategic leadership, in which professionals throughout the organization are genuinely engaged and can influence its culture, ethos and strategic direction, albeit to an extent that is commensurate with their position.
>
> (PricewaterhouseCooper 2007: viii, para.12)

The findings of this exhaustive study are that the quality of school leadership is the second most important determinant of the quality of pupil learning. As the most important element is classroom teaching, it is argued that all teachers should be seen as leaders and developed as such, through helping them to build vision, develop colleagues, think in strategic terms and manage teaching and learning. In a way this is a cyclic development because effective leaders are an influence on the motivation of others which in turn enhances their personal motivation to succeed. The authors found that school leadership has a greater influence where it is most widely distributed providing that it is effectively led and managed at each level.

But delegation is not as simple as it sounds. Gold and Evans (1998) make a clear distinction between professional development which may be necessary to foster delegation and the process of delegation itself, stressing that:

- Beliefs and values about teambuilding and working with people will inform delegation.
- Careful negotiation and listening are necessary.
- Delegation may not necessarily save time as it involves careful planning and training.
- Delegation is not about getting rid of tasks that the leader does not want to do.
- It is important to examine customs about which tasks can be delegated, for example, chairing meetings is a task which can usefully be passed on for developmental purposes.

(adapted from Gold and Evans 1998: 48)

Jones (2005) in a review of effective delegation argues that the role and responsibilities being delegated should be outlined; the nature of the work being assigned should be clearly explained; the delegate should be left to fulfil their role without interference; there should be some 'rewards' to act as motivation; that there does need to be some form of oversight, and then achievement should be evaluated within the performance management structure of the school or college. Jones (2005) also stresses that there are degrees of delegation to be considered by the leader in outlining the accountability procedures for the delegatee – at one end of the spectrum the light touch approach asks the delegatee to 'let me know how things are going', but at the other extreme the delegatee only recommends and action is taken by the leader.

Reflection

Consider a situation in which you have been delegated a role or responsibility. What was your level of motivation to undertake the new task or tasks? How far were the steps outlined above followed through? What effect did this have on your ability to do the job, and to grow personally and professionally? What would you change if you were to ask someone to undertake a delegated role?

Your reflection possibly leads you to see that if the tie between task and development is broken then delegation is simply a form of 'passing the buck'. Successful delegation depends upon identifying the person most likely to gain by fulfilling the function (although this may mean a higher degree of leader supervision); understanding the process of briefing and training, and developing some system of checking progress in meeting personal and institutional needs.

Summary

Using an example of career progress, this chapter has been concerned with the motivation of individuals as it might contribute to their work organizations. We reviewed the 'classical' motivation theories, then considered how they might play out in practice, before looking at delegation and its links with motivation. This leads us into the developing realm of performance management – our next chapter.

Further reading

The following book is a detailed look at the way in which personal motivation can be encouraged and it links into the performance management issues in Chapter 6. It needs some time for reading but it is a very helpful text: Sonnentag, S. (2002) *Psychological Management of Individual Performance.* Chichester: Wiley Blackwell.

However, going from individual to the organization it is worth looking at the following. This is a short book – literally an hour's read – but it does offer some very good ideas in a challenging way!

Gennett, D. (2003) *If You Want It Done Right, You Don't Have To Do It Yourself: The Power of Effective Delegation.* Fresno, CA: Quill Driver Books.

6   Performance management

This chapter is concerned with the way in which performance management is becoming a major element in leadership. It is about agreeing goals and targets for growth of the individual, team or organization and the monitoring of those goals and targets. On occasions it is linked with financial rewards. The way in which it operates will depend a great deal on the culture in which it operates. Performance management undertaken in a collegial, collaborative framework will tend to be developmental, while in a more bureaucratic environment may be seen as judgemental and mainly for purposes of accountability. There are particular links with Chapter 5, as performance management may enhance motivation, by rewarding efforts and setting challenging but exciting targets which might include the delegation of authority. There are also links with Chapter 11 on institutional and individual development, as targets set in performance management may be reached through professional development activities.

Managing performance within the educational institution

For the past century and a half there have been repeated attempts to secure success within schools in the UK by using a range of performance measurement techniques upon teachers. Annual visits by inspectors testing pupil attainment of rote learning in the 'payment by results' systems of the late nineteenth century gave way to more occasional inspections in the early and mid twentieth century; these led to open but generally toothless appraisal systems in the later years of that century before the development of frequent evidence-based inspections under the aegis of Office for Standards in Education (Ofsted) after the Education Act 1988, a system that has influenced inspection regimes in other countries such as New Zealand. However, an amalgam of external and self-evaluative assessment is now operating in many countries where self-governing schools are provided with systems developed to ensure compliance with objectives set by central government. According to the style of the leader, and the context within which leadership operates, there may be an emphasis on the quantitative, scientific or the qualitative, humanistic approaches to assessment, or their use in a pragmatic manner given the person and task involved. Assessment and evaluation have been developed to foster outcomes and educational leadership. League tables and published reports have become the motivation, some would say driving force, for achieving educational success, and distributed leadership is assessed as part of the process.

In considering what this might mean for head teachers, Jennings and Lomas (2003) suggest that the objectives for performance management should be aimed at:

- Creating a closer linkage between school and management systems.
- Developing processes and strategies that improve management practice in raising standards in the classroom.
- Enhancing target setting and review procedures.
- Engineering a rapprochement between the stakeholders to bridge the divide between the conflicting views about the purposes of appraisal and performance management systems for personal development, performance monitoring and reward.

(Jennings and Lomas 2003: 370)

In a summary of the move towards performance management in English schools, Cutler and Waine (2001) outline the legal framework stemming from the Performance Management Framework (Department for Education and Employment (DfEE) 2000), seen as a means of funding and helping schools to improve by supporting and enhancing the work of teachers. It ensures that attention is focused on effective teaching and school leadership which, in turn, benefits pupils, teachers and schools, and thus should become an integral part of the school's culture. This works through a three-stage cycle of:

- *Planning:* team leaders (head teachers, deputy head teachers and senior teachers with management responsibilities) meet with individual teachers to discuss the latter's priorities. These priorities are to include both the needs of pupils, but also the professional priorities of teachers, and objectives are to be agreed for the coming year. The background to such discussion is to be provided by the school development plan, departmental plans and information about the prior attainment of pupils. Discussion of objectives should encompass 'the progress of pupils in the widest sense'.
- *Monitoring:* the teacher and the team leader 'keep progress under review' and take 'supportive action' when it is needed. The agreed objectives will be underpinned by professional development which is seen as a key aspect of the performance management process. Thus examples of 'performance management

objectives' given in the document seek to link 'professional development objectives' with 'pupil progress objectives'.

- *Reviewing:* this is undertaken at the end of the year, and aims to
recognize achievements and identify areas for improvement and
professional development.

(based on Cutler and Waine 2001: 69–70)

Reflection

This three-stage development has been presented as a school activity. Could
it be applied within further and higher education?

In their review Cutler and Waine (2001) argue that while the three-stage
framework offers a link between student achievement and professional
development, there are possible tensions in the emphasis on quantifiable
national targets without reference to greatly variable contextual factors,
and in the top-down setting of targets by local authorities as agents of
central government. These limit the freedom for notionally self-governing
schools to determine their own objectives and further assume that leaders
and led will be in agreement on objectives and approaches within the
schools. Where this tension occurs both motivation and outcomes will be
affected.

Further, should performance be reflected in qualitative or quantitative
ways? Bush and Middlewood (2005) point to the problems of the difficulty of measuring outcomes; of the impact on measured outcomes of
variations in context between and within schools and colleges; of differences in teacher effectiveness in working with differing students; and
of lack of understanding of the process of effective evaluation especially
where insufficient time is allowed for reflection.

To meet these tensions there has been a movement towards the use of
what has become called a balanced scorecard approach. This attempts to
bring together a number of quantifiable and qualitative elements in one
institutional-or project-based performance management system. This can
have elements pertinent to individuals and to the organization as a whole,
offer evolutionary development of objectives and criteria to policy-makers
within the organization.

> The scorecard is intended to help establish agreed goals. These
> will be supported by measurements – and these latter are designed
> to pull people towards the overall objectives, while also assisting
> them in judging progress against these objectives.

(Kaplan and Norton 1996: 325)

An example is the framework currently in use for local authorities in England to self-evaluate their own progress in developing and implementing policies designed to foster succession planning for school leaders. Performance is internally graded according to quantitative data such as the number of leadership course graduates currently seeking senior positions after one, two or three years after graduation, and qualitative assessment of the content of awareness sessions organized for school governors in connection with developing the leadership culture in their schools.

There are problems when attempts are made to look at organizational performance in the same way as individual appraisal. Storey (2002: 329) summarizes the objections to performance management as:

- The challenge that 'management' of virtually any kind presents to the 'professional' status and standing of teachers. This is associated with the issue of desired autonomy and creativity.
- Performance management tends to be regarded as closely tied to performance-related pay schemes.
- Teaching involves such diffuse and tacit skills that it cannot be made subject to the systematization implied by performance management models.
- Initiative fatigue: the perceived excess of initiatives and change programmes emanating from central government – many relating to partial and isolated performance indicators.
- The lack of time in a school system undercut by lack of resources. These objections can basically be contained within two major issues: professionalism and initiative fatigue.

In considering performance review within the higher education context, Taylor (2007) reviewed the development of approaches internationally and concluded that the pursuit of excellence was supported by a variety of appraisal schemes focusing on the quality of personal output:

> Rewards include: promotions based on teaching excellence; teaching awards and prizes; additional pay and/or increments; publicity and events that showcase excellence; and, new titles that ascribe status. Such mechanisms are encouraged by the Funding Councils.
>
> (Taylor 2007: 510)

Such inducements are however fraught with difficulty and Taylor (2007) demonstrates the problems in developing criteria against which excellence can be judged. These will vary according to subject, context and the expectations of the evaluation team. Because of the polarization that occurs within many higher education organizations between teaching and research objectives, it is possible that reward systems favouring research will further debase the teaching function as an area where excellence should be recognized.

To these, and in all areas of performance review, we can also add the danger of stereotyping expected performance with variation between spurious generosity or over-critical views in assessing female or BME or disabled colleague efforts either as individuals or as part of a leadership group (Bush et al. 2005; Coleman 2005).

> ### Reflection
>
> What would be the best approaches to developing a performance management scheme for sceptical participants within a school or college?

Fitzgerald et al. (2003) looked at performance management within New Zealand schools and concluded that there was an overwhelming tension between bureaucratic control and professional autonomy which could be overcome only if there was a much higher degree of local and professional ownership. There have been attempts to achieve this. Two examples, one of monitoring (i.e. concerned with process) and one of evaluation (i.e. concerned with the achievement of aims), offer scope for further development of performance management that is potentially constructive for all participants.

Monitoring – Assessment for Learning (AfL)

Hargreaves (2005) deals with assessment of, or for, learning as an aspect of monitoring in the classroom. She sets out six possible objectives:

- Measuring pupil attainment against stated targets or objectives
- Using assessment to inform the next steps in teaching and learning planning
- As a basis of feedback for improvement
- As evidence for teachers to learn about pupil's learning
- As a basis for children to take some control over their own learning
- As an opportunity to turn assessment into a learning event.

After consideration of varying teacher perspectives of monitoring Hargreaves (2005) concludes that development requires people to think critically about which approaches to learning really satisfy the personal, professional, long-term and holistic purposes for young people's education – thus bringing participants back to the starting point of vision. This

has been investigated by Cooney (2006) considering the introduction of assessment for learning as an activity to be used by teachers to understand where their teaching should lead, and for children to feel fully involved in their own learning. Judging from the children's own accounts of schooling there is clear evidence that they were engaged and active partners in learning. This cooperative approach with implied equality between teacher and taught has an institutional gain with evidence of increased whole staff responsibility for action, and a premium on mutual respect, involvement and a team approach. Underpinning all this is the need for the teachers to feel that they are gaining in terms of satisfaction as a result of enhancing the motivation of pupils – the Together Everyone Achieves More mantra is a spur for all. Effective leadership encourages, enhances and enjoys both the process and product of involvement.

Evaluation – Within School Variation (WSV)

While monitoring is of great importance, there have to be criteria against which organizational enhancement can be measured; it is much more strategic in direction and at the same time offers opportunities for leadership at all levels. This evaluation depends upon there being an openness within a school so that colleagues are prepared to consider how they contribute to the whole. Reynolds (2007) has developed a system for consideration of progress within a single school known as Within School Variation (WSV), comparing the progress of one group against the average for the school as a whole. He notes that inhibitors affecting the introduction of such changes of evaluation might include the following:

- Weak school management that finds it hard to confront the issue and to develop mechanisms to learn from best practice.
- False modesty on the part of effective teachers/departments, perhaps associated with a misplaced egalitarianism that does not reward helping other practitioners who are less effective because this would mean marking the less effective out and labelling them.
- Small schools in which the range of excellence between teachers may be less and therefore more difficult to use, and the one/two-person departments that may make performance evaluation by subject a highly personal activity.
- Budget/time constraints that make it difficult to create these skill sharing systems since they require time, space and buy-out of teaching for observation/debriefing etc.
- The practice of using exceptional individuals as the models for others when the exceptional may often be idiosyncratic, and utilizing their character as much as any distinctive methods. The

exceptional may also be so far in advance of the remainder of the staff in a school that they cannot actually be imitated.

(Reynolds 2007: 15)

Reflection

How might the issues that Reynolds identifies be affected by stereotyping, e.g. of gender or ethnicity?

If you focus upon the effect of stereotyping of all sorts it becomes evident that colleagues find themselves facing cultural barriers which act as inhibitors when a notional team is asked to become more open in sharing practice and more ready to face prejudices. Introducing Within School Variation is difficult but Reynolds (2007) argues that if change is managed well there can be gains. The introduction of WSV-related change requires a systematic audit of individual school's presenting cultures, organizational factors, past attempts (if any) to deal with the issue and indeed the present scale of WSV itself.

Change should be contextually specific to each school, which will each have their own entry points into the WSV area and issues. These could be micro (the issue of variation in coursework marking standards, say) or macro (departmental/academic year variation in pupil outcomes), according to context. The core issue in managing change is to hold on to the necessary collegiality which is needed to collaboratively generate change, while at the same time recognizing the variation within schools by individuals and departments that is necessary to generate professional learning. The gains from such involvement are, however, considerable in that colleagues are more ready to discuss problems openly; there is high quality observation and efficient data collection; there is enhanced collegiality, and as a result greater consistency of practice and in most instances, more satisfactory outcomes.

Reynolds (2007) sees the most significant inhibitor for development to be a desire to cling to the known and what was done in the past and to find excuses for failing to change. This is exacerbated where there are strong micro-political features in the school context and there is opposition to change. There can also be inhibiting contextual features though. For example, Graham-Jolly and Peacock (2000) report on an evaluation of the 'Thousand Schools' project which aimed to improve a thousand disadvantaged schools across South Africa through holistic 'whole school development'. The authors' research in KwaZulu-Natal was based on case study work and conducted within a 'Focus Forum on Evaluation'. They point to certain tensions between local consortia and individual schools. While concluding that 'many teachers and many children benefited from their participation in the Thousand Schools project', they add that 'the troublesome framework conditions of the project' meant that it could not respond creatively to local initiatives and this may well be a problem with the increasing use of self-governing approaches for schools and colleges (Graham-Jolly and Peacock 2000: 401, 404).

Reflection

As you read the outline of a complex situation outlined in the scenario below, think about the motivation given to the business manager by the principal, the effectiveness of the delegation and the way in which performance management was managed.

An MBA student's reflection on the introduction of a revised system of purchasing in a comparatively small college of further education in England offers an example of the way in which performance management may work at individual and organizational levels. It also shows some of the problems arising from the establishment of power centres and from the attitudes of some senior or middle level leaders to those who would like to bring about change, especially if young, female and from non-traditional career paths.

Scenario: Performance management in a college of further education in England

The college offered a range of General Certificate of Secondary Education (GCSE) examination courses for students, vocational courses associated with commerce, agriculture, building trades and general engineering, and some general educational courses such as the 'access course' for adult returners to education.

Each of the three areas of study was led by a middle manager with considerable autonomy but with an interface with senior management through the Board of Studies. The principal had persuaded the governors that the existing senior administrator, Sarah, should be appointed as business manager for the college and this was agreed despite considerable antipathy from the Board of Studies who felt that 'she was going to be in a position of too much power'. However, it was agreed that she should be examining the purchasing procedures and reporting on that.

The principal suggested that this would be the focus of her performance management in the coming year. She could see that purchasing undertaken by three individuals was uneconomic and she persuaded a commercial company to allow her to trial a financial management package and then presented an unthreatening survey of the financial gains from centralized purchases to the Board of Studies. This demonstrated that overall there could be a 22 per cent saving from 'bundling purchases'.

In her performance management review the principal commended the business manager for her strategic planning of the task, for her ability to work with other people without causing dissent, and for her persuasiveness in 'selling the scheme'. Her response was that the change in financial circumstances meant that the departmental heads were prepared to co-operate because their purchases were more important than the perceived autonomy, which was not actually threatened.

Was Sarah put under unfair pressure? She could have been asked to introduce change without the additional worry of a performance management review to consider. Nevertheless, the result was a positive gain for the college and established her new position.

Where performance management has been developed successfully, it generally, has the following characteristics. It operates with vertical structures following lines of leadership or management so that encouragement is given to the downward delegatees and accountability is rendered upwards in the system. It also requires some coherence so that all involved know the rationale for the system, how it operates, how they will be responsible to their line manager, how targets will be established and that contextual elements will be considered. These all require a person-centred approach so that the contribution of the individual to the organization is recognized, supported and celebrated. These require the integration of performance management with professional development resourced in such a way that delegatees are given necessary training and time to undertake their role. In short the system has to be rational, organization wide, linked to national objectives but focused on personal development, and sufficiently tight to give an element of bite – one of the most difficult aspects yet to be faced.

In the scenario above there was an element of serendipity in the co-incidence of a funding problem and the business manager's attempt to change the system. There were problems in the establishment of her performance management objectives with a single focus at that stage in her career within the college. The objective was not comparable with the objectives offered to the departmental heads whose performance was measured in terms of external examination results, attendance rates and retention rates irrespective of contextual factors or educational processes.

Further, there was no definite target for Sarah, who was subsequently told that additional salary payments would be dependent on the system actually delivering financial gains – what might have been an element of real reward was taken from her. The situation could have been demoralizing as the female 'outsider' in a leadership position, attempting to bring about change among a group of established male colleagues. Care should be taken to ensure that individuals who might feel vulnerable in anyway, perhaps because they are perceived as 'outsiders', should receive informed and caring support.

Jones (2005) offers a great deal of helpful information for performance management review sessions and suggests that these should be well prepared by reviewer and participant; warm in nature with clearly outlined objectives for the meeting; offering a structure based upon job description and performance objectives; identifying progress and those areas for future development and then linking these to professional development opportunities and career aspirations before agreeing objectives for the coming year. To this end Jones suggests that these should be directly related to agreed school or college priorities; specific and concise in nature; offering tangible outcomes or measurement; within the teacher's personal control, and achievable, challenging and time framed (Jones 2005: 145).

Reflection

Think back to any performance-related targets you have been given. How far were they realistic and achievable? Was there anything that inhibited the effectiveness of the system within your school or college?

Improvements in organizational systems occur when people are involved and recognize that there is a need for a change of viewpoint or procedures. Where change is seen as advantageous and individuals have ownership, opposition is minimized and people are motivated to fulfil their role(s) in the most effective way so that objectives can be achieved and outcomes enhanced for students. In considering the inhibitors to this we find plentiful research evidence to suggest the complex relationship between diversity, motivation and effective delegation and performance review. Not just directly, as in gender or ethnic stereotyping, but also in the cultural frameworks within which leaders and led function (Mitakavage et al. 2002; Bhattacharya et al. 2003; Bush et al. 2004; Coleman 2005). The difficulties may not be fully recognized – consider for example, the cultural problems inherent in the relationship between male governors and a younger woman head teacher where the chair of governors is responsible for her performance review. Coleman (2007) quotes a woman head, still in her forties, stating that:

> I was constantly challenged by male colleagues in the early years of headship and even described by a governor as 'a mere slip of a girl'. Members of the local community expressed their doubts as to whether I would succeed in the headship.
> (Coleman 2007: 393)

While unsympathetic and uninformed performance review may have negative outcomes, carefully managed and reflective performance review can be a potent addition to the successful leadership of educational organizations.

Summary

This chapter has been concerned with the way in which leaders within schools and colleges utilize performance management to assess personal and group contributions to organizational objectives. In looking at leadership development towards these ends, Avolio (1999) urges four favouring factors. These are the recognition of the vulnerabilities of all colleagues and an understanding of the way in which these can be faced; the encouragement of commitment, not compliance as a driving force; the development of mutual trust, and the ability to put oneself in the position of others within the organization (Avolio 1999: 134). As you think about your own experience you may find that these human factors are evident within your organization, or you may feel that you are caught in a mechanistic culture within which they are unattainable objectives. Much depends upon the way in which people work together. This leads us into the realm of team structure and development discussed in the next chapter.

Further reading

There is limited literature relating to performance management within schools and colleges. The following texts do offer some insight into the theory and practice involved.

This book gives the background to performance management development and shows how it has been used to support work-based pay and institutional development: Reeves, J., Forde, C., O'Brien, J., Smith, P. and Tomlinson, H. (2002) *Performance Management in Education: Improving Practice*. London: Sage.

The policy setting of performance management within education has also been investigated by this book, which looks at the impact of performance management approaches on professionalism and school organization: Gleeson, D. and Husbands, C. (2001) *The Performing School: Managing, Teaching, and Learning in a Performance Culture.* London: Routledge.

7 Working with and through teams

If you think about your work situation, you will realize that there are very few times when you are undertaking something entirely alone; we are all part of a team in some way, indeed most of us are part of several teams, although we often take this for granted. However, schools and colleges can be much more effective if people understand team dynamics, know how they can contribute their full potential to their team and understand the leadership culture within which teams operate.

In this chapter, we first present an illustration of teams at work in a school in Malawi which helps to illustrate the impact of the wider culture on teams. Then we move on to theory and practice related to team development, team membership and team effectiveness.

Scenario: Leading task-based teams at work in Malawi

There have been recent changes relating to curriculum development for primary schools in Malawi. While facing major problems of resourcing, inadequate buildings and a low level of teacher qualification, there are many examples of the implementation of successful change. One example of this is the development of a Life Skills curriculum aimed at inculcating high standards of conduct, positive attitudes, responsible behaviour and sound judgement in the students. While there is guidance from central government in the Primary School Life Skills Syllabus published in Blantyre in 2000, and advisory help at local level, it is a matter for each school to develop and implement its own curriculum policy.

Our concern is with the way in which this was implemented in a large urban primary school with a notional roll of 1200 children taught in ten classes. Of these, two classes are taught in the open. There is considerable professional development for all 15 staff involved. Steven, the principal, argues that he cannot know all the children and that much depends upon the teachers of each class and their capacity to work with the parents and other members of the community to secure whatever resource help is possible. The school works with two assistant principals who are responsible for curriculum development in what would be seen as the infant (years 1–2) and junior (years 3, 4 and 5) sections of the school although this is modified by the local arrangement to cater for pupils who may be behind because of erratic attendance.

Esme looks after the four lower school classes. She sees the development of Life Skills as most effective when the national syllabus is used and urged her four colleagues to spend time developing a 'values led' framework for the curriculum area. She was not prescriptive but asked her colleagues to agree that their teaching would stress 'the need for respect, the improvement of gender attitudes and the recognition and sharing of individual gifts'. The planning team became integrated and held regular meetings and soon lost any concerns with status and power relationships. Their 'adventure' was to secure help from the local community so that a video-recorder could be purchased and use made of materials from the university media library. This meant that they were able to be more innovatory in their pedagogical approach. The team were enthusiastic 'enjoying working together'.

By contrast Martin, responsible for the remaining seven classes (years 6–12) took a different view. He did not involve his colleagues in the same way as Esme and had fewer meetings, which were more formal. He produced copies of the national syllabus for his nine colleagues and at his team meeting at the beginning of the year told his colleagues to use them as the basis of the work with a stress on the impact of HIV/AIDS and factual teaching of human reproduction and the effects of disease on future work and marriage prospects. For him a didactic teaching method was preferred for the students and a set of wall charts was obtained by sponsorship from the local office of a non-governmental organization. The team spent time considering how they might be used and developing a system for their storage, class access and use.

Steven, the principal, although interested in what was happening, made no comment on the team leadership of either Esme or Martin until the end of the first year of the revised curriculum. He was, however, aware that the district Life Skills adviser had reported that 'the lower classes have a positive and open attitude to life skills and see every teaching session as a source of fun ... but with evident concern for each other's needs and a marked decline in bullying'. By contrast she noted that 'the pupils lose some of the zest when they go into the upper classes and although they talked to me about the impact of HIV/AIDS and know how it is transmitted, they seem to be inhibited when talking among themselves'.

Steven realized that effective delegation of his responsibility required further training for Martin in his approach to his team. The staff concerned were not happy with the arrangements: the three women in his team of nine felt that they were being asked to deal with topics which young boys were inclined to treat too lightly, while two young men in the team argued that they were not being allowed to explore some of the issues raised by the pupils because of the need to cover all the syllabus. Their unhappiness was noted by the principal, who sat in on a planning meeting but he decided not to intervene until Martin had had time to re-act. Shortly after that meeting Martin went to an appraisal meeting with the principal. This gave Steven the opportunity to ask him to reflect on the administration of the Life Skills programme. Martin said that the gains were that all teachers were following the same programme, that he knew what they were teaching at any time, and that it had been possible to develop an assessment based on the knowledge shown by pupils. When prompted, he recognized that there 'might be some unhappiness but I have to be in charge', and he agreed that he was nervous of initiating any new methods of teaching in 'such a potentially dangerous subject area'.

Esme also had an appraisal interview at about the same time. She was commended for the lively way in which she had introduced the subject to both staff and pupils and for the way in which her colleagues felt that the change of attitude had had a deep impression on the younger pupils with a marked improvement in attendance.

The Life Skills adviser then met up with Steven to assess the progress of Life Skills teaching throughout the school. Steven outlined his discussions with Martin and Esme and said that he hoped something of Esme's enthusiasm would affect Martin's group. The principal was somewhat surprised, however, when the adviser pointed out that delegation of important matters to teams required a clear shared vision of what was to be achieved, frequent initial and then light touch involvement with the staff carrying new responsibilities, the identification of development needs and an awareness that 'the buck still stops with you'. And Steven thought that he was doing the right thing – he was, but in the wrong way!

(based on an account provided by an overseas MBA student)

Before we look at how the theory and practice of teams and team leadership relate to this scenario, it may be useful to consider the impact of the wider culture on the dynamics of teamwork.

Culture and teams

In the case of the scenario, the teams were operating in a homogenous culture, but in multicultural schools, team members may be drawing on a range of different cultural heritages and this will impact on team effectiveness. It may mean that individuals may be at a disadvantage because of the attitudes of majority groups, power personalities and cultural stereotyping. The work of Hofstede (1991) is helpful here (see Introduction).

The wider culture within which teams operate can have a considerable effect. Shaw (2001: 55–56) identifies the impact from three sources:

- The social environment including gender and ethnic balance and the nature of the community within which the school operates.
- The formal management systems and their impact on cultural groups, e.g. through pay and promotion structure.
- The actions and behaviours of people within the school or college.

For the teams operating in the scenario, there is a hint that there were gender issues in the social environment relating to women teachers discussing HIV/AIDS with adolescent boys. However, the biggest leadership and management issue was the delegation of power from the principal to the team leaders and the way in which they handled that power. There may well have been discomfort on the part of Martin in delegating his power through the team leadership role in a relatively hierarchical culture. The teachers may have been used to rather more formal ways of working with their superiors and unused to the more informal way of operating that was introduced more successfully in the smaller team working with the younger children in the lower classes. It was potentially problematic to attempt to address curriculum development through delegation, without taking full account of the implications of doing this in a somewhat hierarchical and deferential culture.

Groups and teams

We tend to use the terms 'group' and 'team' interchangeably. There is a distinction though where the team is deliberately constructed for a defined purpose and directed in their task. It is generally recognized that whereas groups may be indeterminate and fluid in size, teams are more limited in size and generally more consistent as the basis of effective operation. In the example, the two curriculum teams were longstanding and carrying out the curriculum development as part of their job. In addition, the team leaders in their own ways worked to bring about a sense of shared purpose. Woodcock (1985: 87) argues that teams provide unique opportunities, since 'they can make things happen which would not happen if the team did not exist'. He likens the team to a family characterized by mutual help and support, with coordinated activities, and where commitment is generated, but goes beyond the family concept to point to the learning opportunities, the identification of training and development needs and the evolution of a satisfying, stimulating and enjoyable working environment. There are elements in the scenario above that indicate the way in which groups of people work together. You will have seen that the attitude

of those leading the teachers at each level had a big effect on the way in which the curriculum was implemented and the resulting impact on pupils. There are also insights on the way in which leaders handle the management of those to whom they have delegated responsibility. This is all about the management of teams as distinct from groups of people. Handy and Aitken (1986) argue that although groups can be random, within work situations they tend to exist to achieve purposes and they identify five reasons why individuals participate in them:

- To share in a common activity
- To promote a cause or idea
- To gain status or power
- To have friends and 'belong'
- Because it is part of their job.

All of these are functions of groups. Adair (1986) reflecting on groups in commercial organizations specifies six key factors which make up a group:

- A definable membership
- Group consciousness
- A sense of shared purpose
- Interdependence
- Interaction
- Ability to act in a unitary manner.

When we look at these assertions, it may seem pedantic to attempt a distinction between group and team, but as indicated above, teams tend to be more formally created for a distinct purpose or as a part of a management structure.

Team development

Part of Steven's problem was that the teams were operating without his having given them a clear idea of their remit. Arcaro (1995) argues that teams need to be aware of the constraints inhibiting or fostering their progress. He sees these as related to the economic, cultural, political, structural and personal context within which the team is to develop. In the case of our example, contextual constraints might include the limited financial resources although Esme's team were able to try and raise external funds from the local community. However, there was a potential clash between the more informal style that Esme's team managed to adopt successfully and the rather formal style and deference to authority that

be the style in some sub-Saharan cultures (Harber and Davies 1997), and which characterized Martin's team.

Developing teams means working through problems and coming to a shared understanding. Tuckman (1965) modified by Tuckman and Jensen (1977) provided a model of team development which has been followed since the 1950s because it does seem to represent what occurs. It is a team development model, incorporating five stages:

- *Forming:* This is characterized by uncertainty and anxiety as the team develops and may include the total cooperation of a 'honeymoon period' and then the reality of working with the leader and each other.
- *Storming:* Characterized by conflict and internal dissent as personal characteristics become known, opinions polarize and conflict develops, often with questioning of the basic values and purposes.
- *Norming:* This is characterized by the development of cohesion and satisfaction as members of a 'group' members as issues are resolved, mutual support developed and fundamental ground rules are established so that cooperation begins and communication becomes more effective.
- *Performing:* By this stage there is a central focus on task completion, with interpersonal difficulties resolved and the completion of tasks seen as the driving force for development. At this stage there is an enhanced interpersonal trust and (we hope) a positive energy.

The refinement to the original model was to add a fifth stage which is important given the dynamics of school and college environments where a succession of teams may be needed in order to cope with rapidly changing educational policy implementation. This stage is:

- *Adjourning:* where the team is likely to disband because the task has been achieved or because team members leave. As break-up is anticipated, team members reflect on their time together, preparing themselves for change.

Reflection

Consider a team of which you have been part. How did it match with the Tuckman and Jensen model? Identify those factors which led to any deviation from the model and attempt to ascertain the practice of the team leader.

Gold (1998) has given further consideration to the adjourning stage and suggests that there could be a sixth 'mourning' stage before people are prepared to break with the team of the past and move on to a fresh activity. This depends upon the loyalty developed by individuals to the team while it was working together. In her review of the model overall, Gold (1998) makes the following observations:

- Even one new member can affect the dynamics of the team and it may mean that there is a need for the whole cycle to begin again.
- That said, it is possible for the team leader to import a new member to enhance team effectiveness and it may be worth the adjustment consequent upon this to secure progress.
- The storming stage may be very short lived, especially where potential members know each other and the context very well. It is important that the team leader acts with skill to move the team through the storming stage especially where conflict may be present – and where open discussion could be beneficial.
- Adjourning is helped where there is some planning for the demise of the team so that achievements can be celebrated and an element of closure given to the project.

(Gold 1998: 24)

O'Neill (2003: 219) takes the view that it would be unrealistic to believe that all conflict within a team can actually be eliminated at any stage but that 'to acknowledge the presence of conflict, latent or active, within teamwork is implicitly to make a case for astute, creative orchestration of the relationships, work and membership of the team'. However, differing personalities in teams can cause problems. Arcaro (1995) suggests that these may be minimized if there is general acceptance of a code of conduct including:

- *Commitment:* within the team but also from the sponsoring leadership
- *Mission:* an understanding of what the purpose of the team is to be
- *Objectives:* agreed as being consistent with the mission
- *Trust:* including respect and willingness to invest in each other
- *Shared responsibility:* developed through a true team focus
- *Conflict management:* recognized as an essential within the team
- *Roles and responsibilities:* developed within the team
- *Participation:* seen as an expectation of all participants
- *Communication:* so that all members have a clear record of events.

Where teams are effective they manage complexity, give a rapid response, achieve high motivation, make high quality decisions and develop collective strength. This can result in power struggles where teams can become dominant and then the interrelationships of team leaders within a school or college can be a challenge to the leadership overall.

Adair (1986) examined the dynamics of group functions, and identified three interlocking needs which have to be managed skilfully if progress is to be made. These are:

- Accomplishment of the task
- Smooth working of the team
- Needs of each individual team member.

If we go back to the example of teams in action at the start of this chapter, their task was the introduction of the new curriculum. One team learnt to work well and enthusiastically together and the other was less successful in doing this. There were needs of individuals in the larger team led by Martin that were not being met, particularly those voiced by the three women and the two young men. Where the needs of even one or two members of the team are not met, it is impossible for the team to work as effectively as it might and in some cases team performance can be improved through ensuring that the qualities the individuals bring to the team are complementary.

Team people

The arguments in the previous section lead us to think about the way in which individuals function as team members. Belbin (1993) who was working from a commercial and industrial viewpoint suggests that there may be up to eight types of team participants. These are:

- *Company worker:* turns plans into action in a systematic and efficient manner.
- *Chair:* recognizes the strengths and weaknesses of individuals and uses these to secure the objectives of the team in the best way.
- *Shaper:* shapes team effort by reminding them of objectives and developing the ideas from group discussion.
- *Plant:* offering new ideas and approaches and stimulating new approaches.
- *Resource investigator:* explores and reports on ideas and is often a useful external link.
- *Monitor-evaluator:* analyses problems and evaluates ideas and suggestions.
- *Team-worker:* acts as a support to the rest of the team, often through improved communications or the management of interpersonal relationships.

- *Completer-finisher:* maintains a check on outcomes so that errors are not made, works with unusual attention and promotes a sense of urgency.

Teams with people offering between them all the functions of the Belbin team-workers are more likely to achieve their ends than a team made up of one or two types; for example, too many plants may produce ideas but very little systematic output, while too many completer-finishers may spend more time than is helpful checking detail. Although individuals are usually a best fit with one of these types, we all exhibit a range of qualities and can identify with at least one other type to a lesser extent. This also means that individuals can be coached to take on a different role if a particular quality is missing from the team.

Reflection

Consider the way in which you have worked as a member of a team. From your experience how have teams gained or lost in effectiveness as a result of imbalance of personalities?

We did not have room to outline the complexity of team membership and culture in our case study school, but it seems likely that Esme had a group of like-minded people working together with easy interchange of ideas to achieve their objective, while Martin was working according to a more formal and hierarchical pattern where his team did not engage in discussion but simply did as they were asked. Given the evidence we have, we could guess that Esme was both a chair and a plant, while Martin was also a chair but probably combined that with the less creative monitor-evaluator role. Moss (2008), in a review of the working of a Unesco programme, noted that Australian teams including both school and university participants were most successful where their social interrelationships allowed understanding of differing roles based upon personal strengths.

Cardno (1999) comments that interpersonal challenges can inhibit progress. In a review of progress in a secondary school she notes that defensive patterns of behaviour often go unchallenged, that time constraints get in the way of really sorting issues, that a plethora of interrelated problems may lead to feelings that the team is not able to secure its objectives, and that the chairperson may not be ready to model productive approaches – sometimes the wrong person is undertaking the role. All these point to the need to review both people and practices.

Team practice and effectiveness

Within schools and colleges it is often assumed that teams will operate on the goodwill of the participants and with minimal direction as occurred in the school in Malawi in our example. Martin's team in the scenario might have fared better with more direction. Also in an age where outcomes are required and accountability is expected, teams do have to operate with a degree of formality. To this end Jones (2005) has outlined practices that can contribute to effective organization. He suggests that team leaders should plan team meetings in advance with a clear understanding of objectives and intended outcomes; inform all members of what is under discussion and why; prepare the agenda in a sequential and timed manner; structure the discussion so that progress is maintained, and finally, produce and circulate as necessary a record of the meeting and its outcomes. He also suggests that leaders should be aware of the many ways in which participation can be encouraged including asking for feelings and opinions; paraphrasing to ensure understanding by all the group; asking for examples; checking for consensus; suggesting action; sharing feelings and questioning assumptions. (The topic of meetings is developed in Chapter 8.)

In this, as indeed in all team activities, there may be a need to confront differences. Effective leadership faces this by recognizing that conflict is occurring, rather than ignoring undercurrents and adverse body language, and uses an armoury of strategies to overcome the problems. Failure to do so will lock the team in a 'storming' stage and inhibit progress towards objectives. Handy (1993) argues that many leaders deal with potential conflict by repression or refusing to admit that a problem exists, withdrawal by opting out of the discussion, or rationalization by which the leader learns to live with the situation.

To overcome such difficulties in a positive way it is suggested that team leaders work so that a 'push-pull' approach is avoided and win-win becomes possible (Fisher and Ury 1981; Kennedy 1989). Handy (1993) identifies how underlying problems can inhibit organizational agreement including poor communications and personal and micro-political rivalries. Effective teams manage these by developing an understanding of common goals, an openness about the way in which progress can be made to those goals, and the encouragement of creative discussion of alternative views. Armstrong (1994) highlights four negotiation stages which may emerge within the team:

- *Preparing:* setting objectives, obtaining information and determining strategy.
- *Opening:* revealing a bargaining position.
- *Bargaining:* spotting weaknesses in the other person's case and convincing them of the need to 'move'.
- *Closing:* recognizing the impossibility of further compromise.

The growth and development of leadership teams in primary schools in England is noted by Kelly (2002) in a small-scale qualitative study:

> It is difficult to pinpoint exactly when, historically, primary school management teams became more than just the head and deputy. It is possibly to track my own experiences as a head teacher from a position of commanding leadership (stemming from the historical belief that this was the head's role), to a wider team sharing management, and now to a way of working I might describe as shared leadership. The difference between then and now is to what extent as a head teacher I am willing to both share the power to do things and to some extent, lose overall control.
>
> (Kelly 2002: 2)

In her research, with seven schools, some of the positive developments related to the growth of the leadership teams included:

- Good supportive documentation so that developments were easily tracked
- Clarity about roles and agreement on values and principles
- Care on the part of the head to delegate (and thus motivate) and not 'dump'
- Development of coaching, mentoring and giving feedback.

Everard et al. (2004) suggest that leaders are aware of ways in which promotion of win-win situations can be achieved so that the viewpoint of a dissenter can be accommodated within the discussion but they admit that creating such situations can be difficult because of entrenched personal attitudes and the hidden agenda which often operate in team discussion.

The need for effective teams has been investigated by Johnson et al. (2008) in their work to align the objectives of schools with those of their local authorities or districts. The authors conclude that team approaches are growing in both the teaching and administrative contexts and that there is increasing crossover so that members of teaching teams are working alongside administrators and vice versa. This is beneficial in that there is greater mutual understanding and as a result funding has been gained by schools and professional development approaches enhanced for administrators and there is increasing evidence that schools and districts are working towards similar objectives in collaborative ways.

This would be called a win-win situation but there is evidence that some teams, constituted without due attention to communication of values and objectives to all participants, can be ineffective. Acker et al. (2005) showed this in an unsuccessful attempt by teams responsible for individualized educational programmes for pupils with special needs at schools in the USA. Although the central government advice was that each individual programme should be based upon functional behaviour assessments, many teams were proceeding straight to curriculum intervention on the assumption that they knew what the pupil wanted. Professional development opportunities lasting two or more days appeared to secure a changed procedure and both teachers and pupils gained from programmes based upon evidence-based individual assessment. And so we ask what are the factors making for team effectiveness?

Developing team effectiveness

It can be assumed that perfectly balanced and well-led teams can be highly effective but much depends upon the culture of organizational learning of the school or college and the teams within it. Cardno (1999, 2002) sees barriers to team learning as follows:

> We develop a repertoire of strategies that are consistent with defensive reasoning. For example, we become expert in giving indirect or mixed messages; we cloak negative feedback with a positive opener; we deflect attention from ourselves to the deficiencies of others; we excuse ineffectiveness rather than confronting it; and so on.
>
> Defensiveness is evident in the kind of communication that takes place in organizations when issues surface that are likely to threaten or embarrass individuals or teams. Teams adopt ways of doing things that reflect an ability to engage in game playing to hide error. Individuals perpetuate appropriate cultural games and invent further games to hide the games that are played. Thus, the defensive reasoning of individuals contributes to the emergence of defensive routines that make it difficult for the team to find out what is wrong or what it needs to know. For a team to learn (and to contribute to organizational learning) it must overcome the defensive barriers to learning that are ingrained in both individual and collective behaviour.
>
> (Cardno 1999: 10)

If this defensiveness is to be overcome Cardno argues that teams need to move from discussion as simply stating a point of view, to dialogue which involves negotiation, additions to the pool of common learning and mutually acceptable communication. She concludes:

> When a team practices genuine advocacy (laying out reasoning and thinking for others to see) and inquiry (encouraging others to challenge views and reveal their own assumptions), with the purpose of increasing valid information for all, it is becoming

effective in terms of engaging in productive rather than defensive dialogue.

(Cardno 1999: 12)

Diversity can bring added value to a team that makes it more effective. In a very different context from schools, the boardrooms of the most important American companies, the Fortune 500 Companies, research has shown that previously all-male teams improve performance when made more diverse, in this case by including women, who tend to challenge what is going on:

> We find that women do make a difference in the boardroom. Women bring a collaborative leadership style that benefits board-room dynamics by increasing the amount of listening, social support, and win-win problem-solving. Although women are often collaborative leaders they do not shy away from controversial issues. Many of our informants believe that women are more likely than men to ask tough questions and demand direct and detailed answers. Women also bring new issues and perspectives to the table, broadening the content of boardroom discussions to include the perspectives of multiple stakeholders. Women of color add perspectives that broaden boardroom discussions even further.

(Kramer et al. 2006: 2–3)

As well as gender there will be other aspects of diversity to consider, including age and ethnicity and the resulting implicit power differentials. Individuals bring many dimensions of their identity to a team:

> people hold multiple identities, some culturally marginalized (e.g., women, racial 'minorities', gays and lesbians) and some privileged (e.g., men, Whites, heterosexuals), and that the meaning and impact of each depends in part on the others. Thus, for example, a gay white man and a straight black man are likely to have different experiences of their maleness.

(Ely and Morgan Roberts 2008: 177)

In order to develop effective diverse teams, Shaw (2001) in the context of multicultural teams suggests that leaders should attempt to understand the causes of dissent, offer culturally sensitive professional development to address these issues and then develop culturally sensitive policies which address differences and yet foster collaboration and understanding.

A danger of cultural diversity within teams is the possible development of subgroups but sensitive leadership can support diverse teams to good effect as they are likely to have 'a greater variety of ideas and perspectives and an increased focus on group processes by members' (Thomas

2008: 180). However, it is vital that a shared sense of purpose is developed: 'through focusing on commonalities while allowing individuals to maintain their cultural distinctiveness' (Thomas 2008: 189), thus gaining from the diversity of the team.

Jones (2005) suggests that teams may need to be coached so that they develop effective practices and valid outcomes. He sees coaching as a function of team leaders and stemming from their awareness of the background to the contribution made by team members. Coaching helps individuals to improve their own performance, provides a supportive working environment, encourages members in valuing others, improves communication, and develops organizational effectiveness with the consequent optimization of resource use. That said, though, the team leader has to have a system which enables him or her to appraise participants. While this may work in a generic team, such as a senior leadership team in a school, it is not usually a feature of teams created to solve particular problems. Where team members are offered opportunities to explore their feeling about their membership and effectiveness within the team they may be helped to improve their presentation of ideas, relate to others, listen and communicate and recognize the needs of other participants. The problem is that where behaviours are coached by a team leader there could be allegations that this is being undertaken so that the leader develops power or influence over participants being coached. This may suggest that personal and professional development should be undertaken by competent people outside the team.

Summary

In this chapter we have looked at how culture may affect the ways that teams work, and then gone on to consider team development, the theory of Belbin (1993) on team membership and finally considered team effectiveness, and its development. In Chapter 8 we continue with the focus on meetings which is where much of the life of a team is played out.

Further reading

For a competent overview of theory read: O'Neill, J. (2003) Managing through teams, in L. Kydd, L. Anderson and W. Newton (eds) *Leading People and Teams in Education*. London: Paul Chapman.

For a discussion of the implications of culture on teams read: Shaw, M. (2001) Managing mixed-culture teams in international schools, in S. Blandford and M. Shaw (eds) *Managing International Schools*. London: Routledge-Falmer.

Participants

Charles, the head teacher, aged 46 and in his tenth year as head of the school, is a hands-on leader spending some time teaching each week. He has generally conservative views on school values which can be seen in the way students move about the school, attention to details of uniform and hierarchical management systems.

Edward, the joint deputy head, aged 62 and in his thirtieth year at the school, is responsible for boys' welfare and for special educational needs. He thinks that the school is becoming rather lax.

Anne, the other joint deputy head, aged 46 and in her sixth year at the school, is responsible for girls' welfare and for administration and financial management. She had previously been involved in schools in less favoured areas and stresses the importance of understanding the context of the pupil in any dispute. She is very aware of being the only female in the leadership team.

Peter, assistant head, aged 38, is recently appointed and responsible for pupils in years 10 to 13, i.e. the older section of the school. He feels that the head is too concerned with the external impression given by the school and that the sixth form (senior pupils) could be given greater self-responsibility and so should be allowed freedom in selecting school wear.

The meeting took place in Charles' office and started punctually, although Edward was a little late having supervised the students boarding school buses. Although they had agreed that they should all take turns with minute taking, it often seemed to fall to Anne, confirming her feeling of 'filling the female role'. Charles always took the chair.

Agenda items of the meeting

First, the meeting began with a discussion on musical activities planned for the end of term. Charles said that the head of music was keen to have an end of term carol service at the parish church. This was opposed by Edward (too much of a problem moving the pupils to the church) and Peter (too much formal religion within the school) and favoured by Anne, who argued that it was one of the traditions of the school and that it gave the pupils opportunity to do things within the community. Charles also favoured the activity on the grounds that 'there should be something special to mark the end of term'. With a 2–2 split he said that he had to take the final decision and that the musical activities would go ahead.

Second, the meeting then moved on to consideration of a submission by Peter that the senior two years of pupils (sixth form) should be consulted about uniform issues. Edward became very annoyed and stood firmly by a strict uniform policy. Edward stated that he had been fighting

8   Meetings

The efficiency and health of a team are most evident in meetings and this chapter focuses on meetings, considering their purposes, processes and dynamics and their place within institutional culture. Much of what we considered in Chapter 3 on communication is of relevance here, as meetings are about communication, both oral and written, and the skills of both listening and speaking are integral to the successful meeting process. The extent to which individuals are 'heard' in a meeting may depend on their status.

Meetings can be an extremely effective communication vehicle and a vital component in productive decision-making. Meetings can also be time wasters (see Chapter 9) when they are badly run. They also act as a good indicator of overarching management and organizational approaches as well as the quality of team development. Organizations which value participation tend to have more open and informal meetings than those within a more hierarchical or authoritarian culture. Effective meeting skills help to preserve the clarity of organizational purposes, enabling leaders to 'hover' or 'helicopter' metaphorically above meetings, identifying the processes at work and ensuring interactions remain productive. Both individual and team roles emphasize the way meetings, whether formal or informal, are integral elements in team processes and how, if handled appropriately, they can be major teambuilding vehicles.

Before we consider the purposes and processes of meetings and how they relate to the wider culture of the organization, consider the following scenario.

Scenario: A senior leadership team meeting in a large secondary school in England

The detail that follows is taken from the notes maintained by a head teacher as part of a leadership training exercise in which he was involved. The meeting was a regular timetabled activity held after lessons had finished on Mondays. The agenda was developed by the head during the previous week as issues arose together with an 'any other business' item allowing for colleagues to submit items for discussion.

to maintain the uniform policy over the years and was not inclined to 'give in to the youngsters who seem to be using Peter for their own ends'. At this point, and rather heatedly, Charles said that this was becoming a personal issue and that it looked as if Peter's contribution to policy development was becoming divisive. In his view the school could not rush into a major change without further debate with all the staff and he proposed that the matter be shelved. Peter's response was that there could be no progress, or indeed place, for him, without some acceptance that the school had to move forward.

The final item for the meeting was to seek ideas for the senior leadership team development day in the coming term. Anne proposed further training in examination assessment so that she could be sure that all the team understood changes consequent upon the introduction of new national examinations. Edward said that the time had come for a thorough review of the school rules because the existing 'respect people and respect property code was too open to individual interpretation and didn't help with discipline on the buses'. Charles said that he felt there was need to look at the vision statement for the school as the national and local context was changing. Peter proposed some team role analysis so that 'we can get to understand better the way in which we can work together'. Charles asked for time to consider what had been said, and also to consult the local authority advisory service.

The chair's analysis

At this point the head had observed in his meeting notes:

> We really are faced with a problem. Edward is becoming more difficult and obstinate as time goes on and is constantly undermining any attempt to get vitality into the place ... and his antagonism to Peter is obvious in all we talk about. Peter is clearly feeling that he hasn't got a chance in the school and is clearly looking to me to give him more support than I am at present. Anne has a loyalty to Edward and yet is keen to get the administration sorted as we face the new national systems. As for me – I really believe that we need a new vision for the school, and that is greater than one training day, and so my inclination is to go with Peter and suggest that we have a day looking at our contributions and ways of working as a team.

The outcome

The interaction of both team and meeting management is shown in this recorded research. In the event it was decided to have a training day on team development. Edward said that he thought the time had come for him to retire but he would go along with the development activity, 'although I don't hold out much hope that it will change me'. Anne 're-gretted that we are spending time dealing with airy fairy ideas but it would be a good thing to give Peter his platform'. Peter said that he 'hoped people will see that this is about more than school uniform'. Charles had a long session with the adviser planning the training but asked: 'Is it the way I ran the meeting, or have we really got a problem?'

This meeting is only one example of the way in which this team works together and it illustrates a lot of unresolved conflicts and ambiguity of roles. Charles, the head teacher, is aware that the meeting could have been more productive and that the team is not performing well. He sets up and chairs the meeting, where tensions between members of the team remain unresolved. It appears that the team has become stuck in its development and has not progressed fully to the performing stage (see Chapter 7). Certainly, they have not managed to accommodate their differing stances on what is important in the school. We will continue to consider this example as we look in the rest of the chapter at the purposes and processes of meetings and their connection to the prevailing institutional culture. We will also be considering the dynamic of power relationships in meetings and how they might relate to teambuilding.

Purposes of meetings

The meeting in the example was a regular timetabled meeting of the four people who were the identified leaders of the school. The head teacher was relatively hierarchical in his management style and therefore this team would carry most of the responsibility for the school in contrast to one where a more participative or distributed leadership style was fostered. In an organization with distributed leadership, leadership functions would be dispersed to other teams operating with a flatter management structure rather than a hierarchy. In the school in the scenario, power is centralized and that emphasizes the importance of the team and their meetings. It would therefore be necessary that the senior leadership team met regularly to ensure that they keep abreast of current important issues.

Meetings can be called for a variety of purposes. Everard et al. (2004: 59) identify the following purposes. They may be for:

- Taking decisions
- Collecting views
- Briefing people

- Exchanging information (e.g. in relation to the development of a project)
- Brainstorming
- Investigating a particular problem.

To these could be added purposes for meetings that:

- Instruct or control and where the objectives are those of the manager/leader
- Sell, where an individual tries to persuade others
- Seek advice
- Negotiate or seek a compromise where there are conflicting views
- Support individuals emotionally or for development or by teambuilding.

(based on Williams 1994: 207)

The meeting in the scenario does not fit neatly into any one of those categories, but includes elements of several. It was certainly a decision-taking meeting, with Charles taking a decision on the first item at the meeting and choosing to defer his decision on the third item until he spoke to an adviser. The meeting served to collect the view of the participants on the third item, which had elements of brainstorming, and Peter was aiming to 'sell' his idea of uniform change in the second item. Although there was a need to settle conflicting views, there was little evidence of negotiation towards compromise and certainly no evidence of supporting each other emotionally, or of teambuilding.

Given the hierarchical nature of the school, it is likely that they had a traditional meeting pattern that was not questioned. The senior leadership team was timetabled to meet every Monday after lessons and the head teacher decided on the main agenda items before the meeting. In this context the regular weekly meeting was essential and was built into the system. However, in any organization it might be useful to audit the meetings structure, reflect on the frequency of face to face meetings and look at possible alternatives based on the identified purpose of the meeting.

If a meeting is purely about information giving, then consideration should be given to substituting written communication either in hard copy or electronically. Intranets and virtual learning environments provide opportunities for mutual diaries; notice-boards and ongoing discussions sometimes obviate the need for a face to face meeting.

Meetings can be a rich source of learning. The skills of chairing and minute taking can be learnt and developed, and rotating the chairing of meetings gives a wonderful opportunity for professional development of less experienced team members, if supported by a more senior team member acting as mentor or coach. In the scenario, Charles is always the chair.

If he suggested that other team members might take turns in chairing and minuting, it might improve the meeting and the relationships between team members and help to reduce leadership stereotypes.

Reflection

Think back to the last three meetings in your organization where you have been a participant. In what ways has the purpose of the meeting been inhibited by hidden personal or political agendas?

Processes and procedures of meetings

As well as considering whether the meeting structure is fit for purpose, a factor that should be taken into account when reviewing the pattern of meetings is cost-effectiveness. Where four senior people set aside several hours a week for a leadership team meeting, it is worth considering the cost of their being there, both in terms of their 'daily rate' and in terms of the opportunity cost of what they might have been doing if they were not at the meeting. The efficiency and effectiveness of meetings will be enhanced if they are genuinely needed and if the practical processes of planning, chairing and minuting the meeting are accomplished well.

All meetings should be set up to be productive with tight procedures that ensure efficient follow-up and action, otherwise they are not worth holding, although an exception might be a meeting that has emotional support as its main purpose.

Preparation for the meeting

We have all attended meetings where we felt that we were wasting our time and where we could see no benefit from attending. Good preparation is a key to ensuring that this does not happen. In the scenario, we could not see a clear overall purpose to the meeting. The agenda was prepared without consultation although there was an opportunity for members to raise items under 'any other business'. We do not know if the agenda was available before the meeting but it would have been good practice to make it available.

If all those in attendance are to contribute to the meeting and benefit from it, they need to know in advance what will be on the agenda and to have read the minutes of the previous meeting and any other relevant papers. Although some individuals may put a low priority on this sort of preparation, it is actually both important and urgent (Covey 1989) as it means an individual can add value to a meeting and eliminates the feeling of time being wasted. Ideally, agenda items should be agreed, with items introduced at the meeting by members who first suggested them.

Importance of time and timing

It is also useful to have an indication of time allowed for each item on the agenda and a clear starting and ending time for the meeting. The timing of the meeting during the day and the week will also have an impact. In the scenario, the important leadership meeting takes place at the end of the day when participants may be tired. Long meetings at the end of a working day may be less efficient and, although difficult to avoid, too many will pose difficulties for participants with responsibilities for young children or elder care.

Check the environment for the meeting

We should not forget the importance of the environment for meetings, for example context, layout, seating and refreshments if appropriate, all of which affect the way in which the meeting and its members are perceived to be valued by the institution. The fact that the meeting in the scenario took place in the office of the head teacher, his 'territory', would automatically tend to give him more authority over the meeting.

Chairing the meeting and developing chairing skills

The chairing of meetings is a skill that may need to be learned or improved and it may be worth considering coaching for this. For example, it would be useful to be aware of a range of barriers to clear interpersonal communication in meetings including being aware of differences in value systems and avoiding pre-judging outcomes. Armstrong (1994) argues that effective communications and meetings management skills can be integrated through:

- Taking everyone's views into account
- Ensuring ideas are clearly articulated
- Ensuring information is exchanged
- Ensuring that aims and objectives are coordinated
- Encouraging synergy: collective creativity is greater than individual contributions.

On a practical level, Jones (2005) itemizes the ways in which the chair can help to structure the discussions most effectively:

> Structure the discussion in stages so that all the data and facts come before any interpretations are made, and all the interpretation before a decision on the action. Keep the stages separate. Stop people jumping in or going back over old ground.
>
> (Jones 2005: 91)

Ensuring that everyone has a chance to contribute is one of the key tasks of chairing a meeting. It is easy to presume who knows most about a subject, and we all start with stereotypes and preconceptions about status and power which affect our perceptions of what people are saying. Williams (1994: 209–210) suggests that a researcher or a coach observing meetings could start to analyse the dynamics of the meeting and of the people involved by asking for each issue covered:

- Who speaks on that issue?
- For how long?
- What is the nature of their contribution?
- How effective is their contribution – particularly in helping to achieve the objectives of the meeting?
- What helped progress on the issue?
- What hindered progress on the issue?

William (1994) also suggests that we could ask for each person:

- What did they contribute to the discussion?
- What was the nature of their contribution?
- How did they help in achieving the purposes or objectives of the meeting?
- How did they hinder the achievement of purposes or objectives?

Although it would be unrealistic to try to analyse all meetings in this way, it might be helpful for developmental purposes to adopt this approach from time to time.

A key task for the chair is getting agreement on a decision. Hayes' (1996) study of collaborative decision-making, in which heavy reliance is placed on securing agreement, identifies three strategies for achieving outcomes and maximizing potential for agreement:

- Leader uses a 'pre-decision' which is not open to negotiation, but allows others to comment (disagreement is effectively pre-empted).
- Leader offers several options and participants select one (thus enhancing opportunities for agreement).

- Leader lets all speak, encouraging collegiality and participation (which means leader must then accept the outcome).

In the example at the start of the chapter Charles the head teacher was probably close to using a 'pre-decision' at the meeting and was certainly not taking the third option of encouraging collegiality and participation.

Give everyone an opportunity to speak

Anne, the deputy head, was very aware of being the only female on the team and might have felt, from time to time, sympathy with the common complaint that an idea coming from a woman in a meeting is ignored, and then greeted enthusiastically when voiced by a man. This example is borne out by research undertaken for the Australian Government Publishing Service (Roberts undated [c. 1995]) and the conclusions are endorsed by a meta-review of relevant literature on communication styles of men and women undertaken by Schick-Case (1994).

The Australian research project sought to 'identify behavioural patterns and attitudes which reinforce or impede women's abilities to participate in key decision-making committees' (Roberts undated: 7). It was felt that like most large Australian organizations the university had a preponderance of men in senior positions and that 'the male style of interaction has therefore, become established as the norm' (Roberts undated: 7). As a result 'women who seek to raise a different perspective are often the subject of subtle (and sometimes not so subtle) put-downs' (Roberts undated: 7). Similarly, softly spoken males, or those from a different ethnic background, are considered 'weak' when contrasted with their opposites.

The research included: structured observation of meetings, a questionnaire completed after each meeting to describe experience and perceptions, and follow-up interviews.

The summary of findings stated (Roberts undated: 28):

- There is increased representation of women on the committees but men tend to dominate the meetings taking up between 58 per cent and 86 per cent of speaking time.
- Women see their role as having a responsibility to put forward a range of views to reach a satisfactory outcome. Men see their role differently.
- Women feel that they, more than men, are more likely to be ignored by the chair.
- Women are more likely to raise ideas and question which lead to debate and decision-taking, but are less likely to have their contribution recognized.

- Women report that they are inhibited by the personal and sometimes aggressive nature of debate, but men do not.
- Women report more than men that they are sensitive to paternalism and trivialization of their presence.
- Women are more likely to report lacking confidence than men.
- Women are more likely to feel dissatisfaction with their contribution.
- Confidence, intimidation, participation in debate are all related to the position in the hierarchy and level of experience of meetings.

Although these findings relate mainly to women, note that they were also found to relate to softly spoken men and people from minority ethnic backgrounds, mirroring the power differentials in the wider society. Ely and Morgan Roberts (2008) from a background of organizational theory sum this up:

> Societal power disparities between identity groups are manifested at the personal and interpersonal levels, hindering the effective functioning of culturally diverse teams.
>
> (Ely and Morgan Roberts 2008: 175–176)

The concept of discourse is also useful in considering the extent that individuals participate in a meeting. Discourse is defined as:

> Forms of knowledge, sets of assumptions, expectations, values and ways of explaining the world that govern mainstream cultural practices, including those within organizations.
>
> (Baxter 2006: 155)

Discourses are also linked to sources of power, so that 'all interactions between speakers are interwoven with a web of social and institutional discourses, which act as a means of organizing power relations between these speakers' (Baxter 2006: 156).

Being aware that there are dominant discourses (e.g. of white, middle-class males) would be helpful to the chair of a meeting who wants to ensure that individuals are treated equally and that all voices are heard. (See also Chapter 4 on Communication.)

Minutes and agreed actions

Accurate and helpful minutes are a vital outcome of a meeting, as they provide the foundation for acting on decisions made there. Without a written record it is unlikely that much will actually happen. It is important that responsibility for actions is clearly allocated with an individual and that the carrying out of necessary actions is monitored. Who has final responsibility for checking the minutes? Even though the question of whether they are a true record will be asked at the next meeting, individuals do not always question matters of substance, and the potential for misunderstanding or even misrepresentation always exists particularly for those who were not at the meeting. Written records of agreements (e.g. minutes, aides-mémoires) can be appropriate strategies for limiting misconceptions. However, it is worth considering that they can be 'massaged' and manipulated to control information flows and decision-making. There is a story of a famous chief executive officer of a regional education authority in England who received commiserations from a colleague as they walked from a meeting: 'Things didn't go well for you tonight, did they?' The answer came back, 'You haven't read the minutes yet!'

Reflection

Some people favour a 'blow by blow' account in the record of the minutes. Others prefer a 'conclusions only' approach. What are the comparative advantages of each?

Evaluation and reflection

At the end of a meeting that has run to time, there should be a brief opportunity to reflect on the meeting, the extent to which it has fulfilled its purpose and the roles played by the participants. Any changes arising from these reflections can then be applied at future meetings. The end of the meeting is the time to remind members of actions before the next meeting.

Preparation for the next meeting

Ensure that sufficient dates are set for further meetings as appropriate and that the accurate minutes are sent out in good time for people to read before the next meeting.

Meetings and organizational culture

The way in which people react to one another in meetings and in teams and the conduct of meetings are to some extent products of the culture of the organization as well as the wider national culture (for the Hofstede (1991) dimensions of culture, see Introduction).

Culture can be defined as the sum total of all the aspirations, relationships and practices within an organization. In comments on some pilot work in Washington DC, Deal (1985) speaks of culture as 'the way we do things around here'. This leads to questions about meetings: are they well regulated with a published agenda, firm chairmanship and recorded and distributed minutes (some would argue, a reflection of formality), or are they relaxed, unstructured, and left for participants to remember as they will? This could indicate a culture with devolved responsibility and distributed leadership, or one where ambiguity reigns.

West (1999) has shown the impact of micro-political alliances on school cultures. Such alliances may manifest in meetings where a tension develops between the head teacher as leader attempting to control discussion, and micro-political groups attempting to subvert this through planned intervention with diversionary tactics. Busher (2001: 95) refers to the need for 'informal interpersonal strategies and negotiative processes that allow organizational actors to take account of the broader micro-political and macro-political frameworks' in addition to the rational approaches to management. Head teachers usually see the culture of the school in terms of the way in which values and vision underpin policy and practice, reflecting the work of Staessens and Vandenberghe (1994), but they also admit to a further tension between the ideal of consultative approaches and the reality of control of the debate. For Deal and Peterson (1999: 89) this can lead to 'toxic, organic, and wandering' interactions as negative or positive forces within the school. This can be contrasted with examples of good practice found among 'principled principals' (Gold et al. 2003: 132) where following research in ten schools known to be following good practice, the researchers reported that:

> frequently we were told about the importance of meetings as decision-making spaces and about the amount of information made available to staff. Meetings can be seen as the visible manifestations of a school leader's values system: clear ideals about respecting, transforming, developing and including staff can be evidenced by the importance given to meetings in a school and the way they are run.
>
> (Gold et al. 2003: 132)

You will probably be aware of Handy's (1993) typology of cultures; consider also its implications for the management of meetings:

- *Club orientation:* marked by intricate networks of micro-political groupings and power groups – and a great deal of pre- and post-meeting activity as alliances are formed and broken.

- *Task orientation:* marked by ad hoc matrix organizations designed to solve problems and to get the work done – often through tightly structured agenda and the need to produce outcomes and with teams coming together and then breaking up as soon as the work has been completed.
- *Role orientation:* marked by structuralism and the dominance of bureaucracy – often marked by formal presentations, timed debate and advice to the leader rather than true consultation.

You can see similar implications for meetings in the Bush (2003) typology which follows and which may help to prompt you to find examples of meetings you have experienced where these arrangements prevail.

Reflection

Which of the following models best fit the meetings you regularly attend?

- *Formal models:* these are authoritarian in mood and with strongly hierarchical structures of consultation and decision-making may be bureaucratic, and imposed, or rational and linked to the needs of the school development plan.
- *Collegial models:* these aim to be consensual and with a strong team element in both policy-making and practice and which offer time for debate.
- *Political models:* these are typified by interest groups who negotiate, bargain and form alliances in pursuit of their own objectives. Conflict and vying for power occur. Meetings may be the arena for power struggles or there may be hidden agendas.
- *Subjective models:* where the personal power of individuals inhibits cohesion and the development of whole-school policies and where power politics predominates in the progress of meetings.
- *Ambiguity models:* these are characterized by random and variable practice and often with a marked difference between rhetoric and reality such that meetings are unpredictable, unstructured and often unrecorded.

Summary

Teams frequently operate through meetings and this chapter has concentrated on meetings looking at the dynamics and power relations that might be observed and taking account of equity issues within meetings. The practicalities of meetings have also been considered and finally the style of meeting was contextualized through identifying the links with the culture and leadership style of the organization.

Further reading

For general analysis and practical suggestions read: Everard, K.B., Morris, G. and Wilson, I. (2004) Managing meetings, in *Effective School Management*, 4th edn. London: Paul Chapman.

Jones, J. (2005) Improving the effectiveness of team meetings, in *Management Skills in Schools: A Resource for School Leaders*. London: Paul Chapman.

For a fascinating case study analysing a management meeting from a gendered post-structuralist perspective read: Baxter, J. (2006) Putting gender in its place: A case study on construction speaker identities in a management meeting, in M. Barrett and M. Davidson (eds) *Gender and Communication at Work*. Aldershot: Ashgate.

9   Managing time and stress

The focus in this chapter is partly on you as an individual and partly on you as a manager and leader of others. Your ability to manage your own time and stress will mean that you are able to model good practice. Your sensitivity to the causes and management of stress will strengthen your ability to lead and manage others.

The first section of this chapter is concerned with the cultural concept of time, moving on to a consideration of its management, something which is often related to stress. The focus is then on managing stress as an individual and within the organization and then the potentially stressful impact of education policy. The chapter concludes with a brief look at some aspects of work–life balance.

Conceptualizing time

We perceive time in different ways. We have work time and leisure time. We might prioritize how we spend our time and we might regret 'wasting it'. It can seem slower on occasions for example if we are in hospital, and seems to speed up when we are happy or busy. We are all aware that time seems to go more quickly as we get older. From the point of view of different cultures perhaps the most important difference is whether time is perceived as 'sequential' or 'synchronic'. Time is sequential, where it is seen as a line of events following each other and where we concentrate on one thing at a time, in an orderly manner following a 'critical path'. Time is perceived as synchronic, where commonly people are doing several things at the same time and see that there is more than one way to reach a certain point.

As well as having different views of time in different cultures, there appears to be a distinct difference in the perceptions of time generally held by men and women, with men thinking sequentially: 'past, present and future as passing us in a straight line like a train' and women holding a view of time where 'past, present and future are synchronized and merged within the mind as interactive, parallel processes' (Trompenaars and Hampden-Turner 1997: 234).

On the whole, although of course there are always exceptions, life at work in the Western world follows the 'male model' of the sequential view of time so the differences between these two views of time can lead to frustrating misunderstandings where different cultures meet. In a culture that favours a sequential view, being late for a meeting is rude, while in a culture that is more synchronic, being punctual may be less important than, for example, giving due deference to people of a higher status who you encounter on the way to the meeting. With regard to the different cultural attitudes to punctuality:

> Meeting times may be approximate in synchronic cultures. The range is from 15 minutes in Latin Europe, to part or all of a day in the Middle East and Africa. Given the fact that most of those with appointments to meet are running other activities in parallel, any waiting involved is not onerous and later arrival may often even be a convenience, allowing some time for unplanned activities.
>
> (Trompenaars and Hampden-Turner 1997: 125)

Even the view of planning will be affected by whether the culture is sequential or synchronic. For example in the USA (sequential) business is dominated by quarterly reports and planning is usually only a few years ahead at most, whereas the Japanese (synchronic) view of a business plan may extend to 50 or 100 years (Trompenaars and Hampden-Turner 1997: 128). It is helpful to know that different cultural conceptualizations of time exist, although in the interests of smooth working practice, an 'outsider' might need to adapt to the norms of the country where he or she is working or at the very least be aware of how conceptions of time may differ if they are to avoid frustration.

Within the world of education, there tends to be a recognizable framework for time:

- *Macro time:* the structure of the year, the semester, the term
- *Micro time:* details of timetable, or the length of a lesson in the school, or a module or unit in higher education.

In addition to the cultural norms within which we live there are personal notions of time covering private and personal and domestic time. Of course, we do not always clearly separate the private and domestic use of time from work time and our attitudes to time management are likely to affect every aspect of our lives. For example, in relation to both possessions and to what you do: 'many people are natural hoarders, live by habit, don't want to be left out or can't say "no". The result for most is that there are just too many commitments' (Allard 1988: 32).

Time management

If the feeling of having too many commitments and not enough time is one that is familiar to you, it will probably help to:

- Analyse how you use your time
- Identify time-wasters
- Plan: long, medium and short term.

Analyse how you use your time

To analyse your time it is useful to keep a time log or a diary. Although you may think you know how you spend your time, when you do log it properly, it is often revealing. Keeping a log is easier if you identify types of activities or priorities and code them, e.g. 'M' for meetings, 'T' for teaching.

As an example, one particular primary school principal's work over five working days in an urban school in Nicosia, Cyprus, was recorded and then divided into four categories (Kasoulides and Pashiardis 2004). The detail is omitted here, but the first two categories identify proportions of time spent alone or with others. The second two identify the manner in which the time is spent:

- Alone about 30 per cent of the time mainly dealing with paper-work, and preparation for teaching and meetings.
- Communication with others face to face, mainly students and teachers (58 per cent of the time), and through correspondence and the telephone (15 per cent). Direct contact with parents accounted for just over 3 per cent of the time.
- Walking around – nearly half the time was spent in his office and only just over half outside, mainly in the classroom for teaching, or in the staff room, or working with the secretary.
- Interruptions, including following up on 'urgent' things. For example, after a telephone call about a child with special educational needs, the principal stopped what he had been doing and went to talk to the special educational needs teacher about the child. The secretary also interrupted to talk about correspondence.

The conclusions from the study are:

- The principal has more freedom for time management than anyone else (confirmed by other research projects).
- The work of the principal is complex.
- There are no 'recipes' for time management, but it is important to be vigilant for those things which may be labelled 'urgent'.

- Thoughtful planning and the classification of activities can help the principal to cope.
- The effective management of time is inherent in the work of effective principals.

Identify time-wasters

Time-wasters, or 'time thieves' as Jones (2005) calls them, include holding and attending poorly managed meetings, allowing interruptions, not planning, not being able to say 'no' and allowing paperwork to pile up so that you waste time looking for important documents. You will be able to identify your own particular versions of these time-wasters. If it is paperwork that causes you problems, Adair (1988) recommends handling each piece of paper only once. If that is not possible, they can be sorted into:

- *For action:* complete the action or mark it with the action to be done.
- *For information:* read, file, throw away or pass on.
- *For reading:* keep for marginal time.
- *For waste paper:* if it fits into none of the other categories.

The advent of emails has added a new type of potential time-waster and it may be wise to apply rules such as accessing them only at certain times of the day; carefully archiving those that might be needed again; and ensuring that those that need action are dealt with immediately or marked so that they are not 'lost'.

Plan: long, medium and short term

Lack of planning leads to wasting time, and planning effectively in the short, medium and long term can be very helpful. Long-term planning could include setting goals for life, both personal and professional, and considering your values as we have discussed in earlier chapters. Medium-term planning might be for the next year or two, while short-term planning could be through your diary, or by having a daily list with which you start and end the day. In doing this remember the distinction made by Covey (1989) between what is urgent and what is important. We have already considered this in respect of the Cypriot principal above, and in respect of meetings in Chapter 8. Urgent tasks should not continually 'crowd' out what is important, and what is important can be identified through consideration of your values. Identifying important tasks and giving them time can also help to reduce stress. Wilkinson (1992) coins the term 'administrivia' to sum up those activities that are trivial and unimportant but which can take up too much of a manager's time. Delegation is obviously important and relevant here.

Reflection

Thinking about your daily routine, can you identify your own particular 'time bandits'? Is there anything you can change – that you can downgrade from urgent, that you could ask someone else to do or that you actually don't need to do at all?

Time and teaching

Teachers experience time somewhat differently to other professionals. Galton and MacBeath (2008), looking at workload in schools in England, quote the PricewaterhouseCooper (2001) survey which showed that teachers without management commitments work on average the same length of working week as managers and professionals in other areas, that is 45 hours a week. However, in term time they work around 52 hours a week and experience a much more intense workload than individuals in other walks of life. In addition teachers are likely to spend time on work outside the normal working day of 9 to 5. The same pattern of work is applicable in colleges so that during term time teachers and lecturers are likely to feel pressure and an excessive workload. We will look at this area in more detail in relation to the policy context of education later in the chapter, but first look at stress as it relates to an individual teacher in a primary school.

Stress and work

Scenario: Stress in an English primary school

Miss Jane Jones is a 45-year-old Key Stage 2 mathematics specialist in a large primary school in an English market town. She has been at the school ever since leaving college 21 years ago and has always been responsible for the 25 or so 8–9-year-old pupils. She entered the school with a good deal of enthusiasm and enrolled in a two-year MA course at the local university. This was satisfactorily completed and her then head teacher (an avuncular, easy-going male) suggested that after getting a little more experience, she should look for promotion. However, at that time she had complex personal problems, losing her father in tragic circumstances and then experiencing a broken relationship. A pattern of occasional absence emerged but the head felt that 'given time all will be well'.

There was a change of head teacher in the school and a decision was made by the head and the other staff that they would all take a curricular responsibility. Jane agreed to look after mathematics, her college specialism. The head teacher noted that Jane was working long hours, coming into the school early in the morning and then staying to cope with marking until late evening on three days each week. She also noticed that every three or four weeks Jane was absent for two or three days with minor illnesses and that other colleagues had commented upon her irritability and unwillingness to join in school social activities, and that there were increasing social behaviour problems with children from her class.

The head teacher spoke to Jane. Jane denied that she was under pressure, said that all was well, and that the real difficulty was that the calibre of children coming through her class had declined across the years. 'They just aren't as responsive as they used to be.' The head teacher suggested that Jane should try to prioritize what she did each week and term but Jane retorted: 'All of that sounds like some sort of weakness on my part and as far as I am concerned it is the system rather than me having problems.'

Two terms later there had been little improvement and Jane was gaining a reputation as a cynic. In the words of one colleague Jane was 'not the person I can go and talk to about mathematics as I should . . . she is only concerned with counting protractors and says that she has no interest in seeing what I am doing'. Another recently appointed college leaver went to the head in tears because: 'I had hoped that Jane would give me some help with the new curriculum planning we have to do but her response was that I should make my own way.' There were also complaints from parents about the lack of enthusiasm felt by their children, and comments from governors about Jane's manner. The head teacher felt that drastic action should be taken.

The action was precipitated by an Ofsted inspection. The inspectors commented favourably upon the orderliness of Jane's classroom, on her ability to deliver the curriculum effectively, and on her meticulous record-keeping. However, they noted: 'Just at the stage where children should be able to discuss ideas, offer opinion and share in their work, they seem to be cowed and afraid of doing the wrong thing.' Further they noted that there had been considerable work in the classification of mathematics resources and that there was a good grid showing the relationship between curriculum objectives and available materials, but the staff appeared not to have discussed some of the major issues connected with the more creative and exploratory new mathematics programme.

Maths was not the only area where there was criticism and the school was then put into special measures (worrying for the school, but a designation that ensures considerable local authority assistance and time in which to improve to an acceptable national standard). Jane had a bad bout of illness and was away from school for five weeks. During this time falling rolls had resulted in the need to shed a member of staff and Jane was convinced that her record would result in her nomination as the one to be declared redundant. The head teacher visited her at home and took a bunch of flowers from the staff and told her that all staff would be considered for redundancy but that the process would not take place until she was able to return to school so that there was absolute equality of opportunity.

When the process occurred all staff were interviewed and in accordance with the redundancy policy prepared by the governors, the most recent appointment was declared redundant (although she was subsequently retained after an unexpected rise in recruitment!).

Having been retained, Jane appeared to develop a more positive attitude and in an appraisal interview agreed that although she was just about able to cope with her workload, she was focusing on the wrong things. The head teacher suggested that one of her colleagues from another school should act as mentor for Jane, ostensibly as mathematics curriculum leader, but in all respects as a class teacher as well. The funding for mentoring help was used in such a way that Jane was promised support each Wednesday for ten weeks.

At the first meeting, the mentor not only probed Jane's workload but also uncovered the many problems that Jane had been keeping to herself over the years. The impact of failed promotion attempts, the loss of the fatherly head, the frustration when her meticulousness was questioned, and her feeling of inadequacy in a changed situation all came to the surface. It was agreed that Jane had been very lucky in that her post and her job were secure but that, with no prospect of future promotion given her recent professional history, she had to make considerable improvements within her existing situation. She also agreed to keep a work diary recording her feelings on a daily basis. When this was clarified the mentor suggested that they should work on seven topics in the coming weeks. These were:

- Developing alternative approaches so that the children were more relaxed.
- Meeting up with all the staff to ascertain what they needed from the mathematics coordinator.
- Developing a maths strategy for the school with an emphasis on supporting colleagues.
- Putting the support for colleagues into effect so that they felt helped by occasional visits from Jane.
- Making use of three hours per week of the time of a classroom assistant so that she coped with the administration of the mathematics materials.
- Re-examining the work diary prepared by Jane at the start of the support and developing a critical view of priorities and their solution.

- Re-examining Jane's personal career prospects so that she could maximize her skills to prepare for promotion if any opportunity was locally available.

Three terms later there was a further Ofsted inspection. Jane was praised for the creativity shown in supporting her colleagues, for the lively example she was giving in developing resources, and for the use of classroom assistant time. Two terms later Jane was approached by the head and encouraged to apply for a deputy head post in a neighbouring school. In her reference the head was honest about Jane's past history but concluded that:

> She has had her problems but now uses her time more effectively, and feeling under less pressure has time to be part of the staff badminton group. As she has coped with stress she has also become more open with colleagues and is valued by parents as a class teacher giving support and encouragement to her children . . . indeed, she no longer has bouts of absence, and says that teaching is fun.
>
> (based on a real life situation as
> recorded by the school consultant)

In this scenario, an initially promising teacher developed problems in managing her working life. Although the head teacher was kindly disposed towards the staff, there did not appear to be any internal 'support' mechanisms to help her talk through her problems. Her stress levels were such that her relationships with her colleagues were impaired and her own health was suffering. Her innate concern with detail led her to concentrate on things that were necessary (mapping the resources) but not of high importance (offering clear guidance to colleagues on the mathematics curriculum and pedagogy). It was only when appraisal led to sympathetic mentoring, after the shock of the Ofsted report, that her problems were addressed and dealt with. Some of the pressures listed by Bubb and Earley (2004: 10–11) from the Teacher Support Network survey include: poor workplace environments; excessive working time and workload; lack of personal fulfilment and poor career prospects; internal politics; excessive bureaucracy; poor communication; low morale; resistance to change or excessive change and a blame culture. Most of these applied to Jane in some way, with the blame culture appearing in the form of a school inspection that publicly identified weaknesses.

But is stress always a negative force? Stress is not an event or a circumstance, but a response to them. The degree of stress that an experience causes is related to the intensity of the demand for adjustment or adaptation. The stress reaction is basically that of 'fight or flight', so that the adrenaline rush that an event perceived as stressful may cause, primes the body and mind and leads to physical symptoms such as increased heart rate.

Technically speaking there are positive as well as negative types of stress. Crawford (1997: 115) identifies four types:

- Hyperstress or too much stress
- Distress or bad stress
- Hypostress or understress
- Eustress or good stress.

Both too much and too little stress can be negative. However, a certain amount of eustress, or perhaps we might call it 'pressure', is needed to ensure that we are performing in a way that challenges us rather than leaving us frustrated in our work.

Stress that is experienced negatively has implications and repercussions for the individual and for the organization. Stress may also be increased through the impact of educational policy working at the national and international level.

Individual stress

In the scenario Jane was experiencing individual stress. Her way of coping was to take time off for ill health and to sublimate her stress in keeping immaculate records. Administrative tasks were done impeccably but she was unable to deal with the parts of the job that she perceived as more difficult, that is dealing with people, both colleagues and students. In Jane's case she was able to work through her issues by keeping a diary which allowed her to pinpoint what she found stressful and then by talking through her problems with a sympathetic mentor. Even if a mentor is not provided or available, individuals can still stop and analyse their situation, trying to define what the problems may be and thinking of alternative ways of dealing with them. The following comments addressed to teachers from the Health and Safety Commission (HSC) (1990: 23) may be appropriate in analysing an individual's stressful situation:

- Does stress arise because your own expectations of yourself and/or others are not met? If so, reappraisal, recognizing and modifying unrealistic expectations, establishing attainable goals for yourself and your pupils, accepting your own limitations and avoiding over-involvement in teaching, may help.
- In some cases, it is known that a particular occasion is likely to be stressful. In this case, 'anticipatory coping' (e.g. preparation, planning, mental rehearsal) will help to reduce anxiety and increase confidence.

- Workload management, for example setting priorities, delegation, time management, recognition that some workload is self-imposed, being realistic about how much can be done.
- If an acute conflict arises, delay, detachment, avoidance or a cooling off period may be helpful short-term measures.
- Monitoring one's own thoughts and behaviours under stress and learning to recognize unhelpful and self-defeating responses reduces vulnerability. Similarly, maintaining a sense of humour and trying to keep things in proportion always helps.

There is no doubt that various individuals' reactions to stress will differ. For example there is a common differentiation of people into personality types A and B. Travers and Cooper (1996) indicate that Type A people are much more likely to experience stress diseases such as coronary heart disease. They identify a Type A person as one who will:

- Work long hours under deadlines and conditions of overload.
- Take work home on evenings and at weekends being unable to relax.
- Cut holidays short.
- Compete with themselves and others and set themselves very high standards.
- Feel frustration at work.
- Can be irritable with others.
- Feel misunderstood by their managers.

It is likely that Jane in the scenario was a Type A person. Taking the advice from the HSC, modifying expectations, managing workload, planning, and monitoring your thoughts as Jane did with her diary are helpful in managing stress as an individual.

Learning can take place through reflection leading to self-understanding. For example, Ostell and Oakland (1995), who studied head teacher stress and health, identify the importance of awareness raising and self-knowledge and the elimination of what they term 'absolutist' thinking which reflects 'irrational expectations, unrealistic standards and low tolerance of their own and/or other people's shortcomings'. Training is likely to be useful to move towards 'more realistic expectations and standards, a tolerant attitude towards themselves, others or the environment' (Ostell and Oakland 1995: 189).

In extreme circumstances an individual with a long buildup of stress may experience what is known as 'burnout'. This is described by Crawford (1997) as where an individual

> finds his or her emotional resources exhausted and he or she may feel undervalued or worthless. The only way for this individual

to go is downward . . . burnout happens to all kinds of individuals when a situation arises that they cannot resolve by their usual coping strategies.

(Crawford 1997: 118–119)

Individuals often react to stress by first seeking palliative measures, which can include drinking, smoking and overeating. More positive reactions and practical ways of coping include building regular exercise into your routine, developing other interests and addressing specific problems such as a poor sleeping habit.

Reflection

Do you recognize when you are stressed? What measures do you take to minimize your stress? Are there additional measures that you might adopt?

Although one individual may be more predisposed to stress than another, and individuals can take steps to manage their own stress, there are still causes of stress that are relevant to the organization as a whole and where leaders and managers can work towards counteracting endemic stress levels.

Organizations and stress

Management and leadership style and its influence on the culture of the organization influence the organizational approach to stress. Values underpin the style and culture of the organization and affect how individuals are treated. As we have seen in earlier chapters, agreement on values and the implications that they may have for structures can then underpin important leadership and management activities such as:

- Induction and mentoring
- Professional development
- The pleasantness of the physical work environment
- Communications
- Teamwork.

In an open, supportive culture discussion about potentially stressful situations can take place and policies and procedures can be developed to deal with them. In the scenario at the start of the chapter, both the first and second head teachers appeared to be fair and well disposed to Jane, but the culture of the school did not allow open discussion of the apparent problems and there was no system to support the individual. It was only after the inspection precipitated a crisis that mentoring was introduced. It is important for managers to recognize the responsibility that the organization carries towards its members. As Crawford (1997: 119) states: 'Blaming the individual is an easy way for an organization to avoid tackling the real problem. . . . Those in management positions need to evolve structures to listen, support and help.' Jones (2005: 32) comments on the importance of team leaders finding the right balance between support and challenge if they are going to get the best from their team. The right sort of 'stress' as in positively applied pressure helps the individual to function efficiently and be motivated.

A study of the stress experienced by principals of kindergartens in Macau looked for causes of stress and the extent to which support from their supervisors helped or made the situation more stressful (Kwok and Wai 2005). The research showed that they were coping quite well with stress but that it was things over which they had least control where they felt most stressed. These were the recruitment of sufficient new students and balancing the budget, which in itself depended on recruitment. Emotional support offered by their supervisors was found to be effective in reducing their stress and it was hypothesized that as well as helping to:

> smooth the negative emotions the principals were experiencing. It is also plausible that emotional support from one's supervisor was perceived as an indication that the supervisor was not or would not put the blame of insufficient enrolment onto the principals.
>   (Kwok and Wai 2005: 192)

Managing stress is certainly not a simple and straightforward matter. In this example it was emotional rather than informational support from a superior that was most effective. Although aspects of the findings may relate specifically to Macau, the stress on recruiting pupils and balancing the budget are important in many countries including the UK where competition between pupils for schools has been the norm since the late 1980s and where funding is linked to pupil numbers.

The wider policy context and stress

Policy changes in education may have a particular role to play in stressing professionals in education. Working in a managerial atmosphere where accountability is publicly demanded through inspection and targets, teachers, lecturers and others may feel levels of stress that are hard for the individual school or other educational organization to counter. Teachers may be stressed because they are being asked to work in ways that do not accord with their values and beliefs about education. Combinations of individual, institutional and national factors may need to be unpicked to identify the causes of stress.

Overloading and stress related to time management were noted earlier in the chapter. Reasons that teachers in England identified for this type of stress included: the impact of educational change on the lives of the teachers, the non-teaching tasks, the increased paperwork linked to greater accountability, covering for absent colleagues, dealing with government initiatives and poor planning in the school (Bubb and Earley 2004: 8–9). The remodelling of the workforce in England recognizes that there are aspects of teachers' jobs that can be better done by others. These include many administrative tasks, invigilation of examinations, a limit on covering for absent teachers and guaranteed lesson planning time for teachers and leadership time for heads. However, in the report on remodelling (Ofsted 2004; Galton and MacBeath 2008), it was often found that heads felt that workloads had not decreased. For example, although some of the secondary school head teachers had increased the size of the senior leadership teams and delegated more responsibilities, they had also taken on some additional administrative tasks to provide their teachers with more time. In the primary schools, it seemed that heads were reluctant to delegate responsibilities, and many of them took on all the performance management meetings for their staff.

Despite some improvement in working hours and the removal of administrative and other tasks from teachers the nature of the work is still demanding. To a large extent the causes of the long hours of work, at least during term time, lie outside the control of the individual teacher or leader in the school.

Troman (2003) carried out qualitative research with 20 teachers who had a range of experience and seniority in England; he also carried out two in-depth case studies looking at stress. In some cases, as with Jane in our scenario, stress was carried over from home. He gives the example where stress arising from a problematic relationship at home contributes to the stress that is being felt at work and vice versa.

More generally, teachers recognized the importance of support emanating from the leadership of the institution, but they did not always feel that they received it. They felt that the intensification of work brought about by policies which make the workplace more managerial, target driven and accountable meant that there were less opportunities for mutual support or support from their leaders. Troman (2003: 179) refers to the "official" distrust of teachers embodied in the new accountability systems' being a source of stress. In particular he puts the blame for this on the Ofsted system of inspection. The conclusion was that:

> Not all of the teachers in this study worked at schools in which distrust had become physically and emotionally damaging. Some enjoyed positive personal and collegial relationships in their work. However, the majority did not.
>
> (Troman 2003: 181)

The combination of external pressure and the increase in accountability and work intensification puts pressure on leaders and managers in schools which make it difficult to manage potentially stressful situations. Bottery (2004: 12–13) recognizes that there are many principled and visionary educationalists, but that the stresses and strains of leading in education and the intensification of work has made life more difficult and this has led to a shortage of potential leaders, certainly throughout the Western world (he quotes studies in the UK, Canada, Australia and the USA). Similar issues are noted by Galton and MacBeath (2008) in relation to these countries and also Hong Kong and New Zealand and similar tensions felt by head teachers in Iceland (Lárusdóttir 2008) in Chapter 4 have already been noted.

Stress and emotions are interlinked and emotions relating to educational leadership and management are considered in more detail in Chapter 10. In a study of individual teachers in 15 Canadian elementary and secondary schools, Hargreaves (2004) focused on their emotional responses to change. The changes that were referred to were both those that were externally imposed (mainly by government) and those that were internally initiated. It was found that the majority of the teachers experienced negative emotions, and presumably more stress, in relation to externally directed change. 'After frustration, anger and annoyance were the most commonly named [emotions]' (Hargreaves 2004: 296). Hargreaves notes that the women tended to be different from the men in their reactions: 'where men tend to turn anger and frustration outwards and blame others, while women turn negative emotions inwards and blame themselves' (Hargreaves 2004: 296). Self-initiated change brought about positive responses even where the change had actually arisen from one that was externally imposed initially. The implication for leadership is that:

> It is less important whether change is external or internal in its point of origin than whether the change process is inclusive or exclusive of teachers' purposes, passions and professional classroom judgement.
>
> (Hargreaves 2004: 306)

This implies that those in charge of educational organizations may act as gatekeepers and mitigate the impact and question the nature of national policy, challenging it when it conflicts with their values. An assessment by Hammersley-Fletcher and Adnett (2009) of the workforce remodelling in England came to a similar conclusion. Although they concluded that 'much of the activity around remodelling is largely acting to support the status-quo', there were head teachers and senior management teams who were using the initiative to 'challenge and rethink educational practice and leadership' (Hammersley-Fletcher and Adnett 2009: 195) and were involving staff fully in this.

The external policy context affects work in educational organizations, but the 'outside world' also impinges on work in educational organizations as individuals try to find an acceptable balance between the demands and interests of their work and their life outside the world of work.

Work–life balance

Part of the remodelling of the school workforce in England, referred to above, was that 'provision must be made for teachers and head teachers to enjoy a reasonable work–life balance' (Bubb and Earley 2004: 17). Galton and MacBeath (2008: 114) comment that the remodelling 'has proved to be something of a palliative', but that it has not really affected the work–life balance of head teachers, of teaching assistants, who have taken on many of the duties that teachers have been able to relinquish, or of teachers themselves.

That may be the context, but for each individual, family and work responsibilities are continually changing so that finding the right balance is not an easy process, and probably requires ongoing negotiation on the part of individuals, their families and their places of work. In England, the legal context is changing, giving more attention to the needs of individuals and families. People who have disabilities or who are older may need flexibility and/or part-time work. Our attitude to work–life balance is changing, with men and women seeking to play a full part in both family life and work. There are tremendous changes starting to take place in domestic life, but at this stage it is normal for the larger weight of domestic responsibility to be taken by the mother in a family where there is a child or children. This may mean that women in work are particularly subject to tensions related to work–life balance, although findings from the London Business School (Gratton et al. 2007) make a counter-claim that it is young men who work long hours and who tend to miss out most on family life while young women make choices that probably put family first.

In research on women and men head teachers and gender in England, Coleman (2005) found evidence of women struggling with a dual role and of men regretting that they could not spend more time with their family. However, overall the work–life balance issues were felt more by the women. The main issues that arose were as follows:

- Marriage and partnerships seemed more problematic for the women. The women head teachers were much more likely to be single, divorced or separated than the men.
- It seemed that many of the women were making choices between career and having a child or children. Only 60 per cent of the women had children compared with 90 per cent of the men.
- Most of the men had partners who took the major role regarding home and child care while many of the women carried the major responsibility for running the home and for child care in addition to their work responsibilities.

Women who take on leadership roles in education seem to be making choices about family life, particularly about having children, and are more likely to be single, divorced or separated. Women in leadership roles are more likely to take responsibility for most of the domestic areas of life. Even in countries where it is common for professional women to have paid assistance, such as Singapore or Hong Kong, evidence indicates that they still take responsibility for the running of the household (Morriss et al. 1999).

Work–life balance not only is problematic for the individual, but also raises issues about the leadership values of an organization. In a research project on women head teachers and networks, it seemed that having experienced the tensions of combining work with having children, the women tended to be very aware of these issues and were quite creative about finding solutions. One stated:

> I never say 'no' [to staff requests for family-related absence]. Staff who have little ones ask if they can go and see them in a nativity play. We get the ones with children to cover for each other. It's about being woman friendly and understanding. Job shares, part-time work. We also do the same for fathers.
>
> (Coleman 2009b)

Flexibility in sharing roles and working part-time give more freedom to find a balance in life. Work–life balance is not just about combining the responsibilities for children or for ageing relatives with paid work. It is also about having fun and finding a balance of hobbies and interests and exercise. The right balance in life will help reduce stress and improve your contribution to work.

Reflection

What is the right balance for me? Do I have a good balance of work, and personal commitments?

Summary

This chapter has focused on the individual and how people might manage their time. The need for time management can in itself be a cause of stress, and this and other aspects of stress and its management were addressed. Not all stress is negative and leading and managing people is to some extent a matter of ensuring the right level of challenge and support. Although the individual features in this chapter, the way that the organization is led and managed can both create and alleviate the stress of those working within it. However, it can be difficult for both individuals and their organizations to deal with the stress that has arisen from recent policy initiatives that hold educational institutions up to blame.

The well-being of individuals within the educational organization is linked to work–life balance, and this still tends to be a particular issue for women.

Further reading

Practical issues and their management in an English context are well covered in: Bubb, S. and Earley, P. (2004) *Managing Teacher Workload: Work–Life Balance and Wellbeing*. London: Paul Chapman.

For further fascinating details about culture and time see: Trompenaars, F. and Hampden-Turner, C. (1997) How we manage time, in *Riding the Waves of Culture*. London: Nicholas Brealey.

For practical information about stress, the individual and the organization see: *Work-Related Stress: Together We Can Tackle It*. Available at www.hse.gov.uk/stress/index.htm (accessed 15 October 2009).

10 Developing understanding of emotion and leadership

Megan Crawford

> *Emotion functions as a prism through which we may reconstruct what is often invisible or unconscious – what we must have wished, must have expected, must have seen or imagined to be true in the situation.*
> (Hochschild 1983: 246)

This chapter starts by considering the relationship of emotion to leadership. Emotion is a huge field of study, and this chapter presents only a few of the approaches particularly relevant to those who work in education. Following some definitions, a scenario, drawn from my research in England (Crawford 2009), leads into a fuller discussion of these approaches. It has been suggested (Lupton 1998) that it is helpful to view emotions as either socially constructed or inherent. Emotions as inherent are concerned with the self, and emotions as socially constructed are based on that dynamic interaction with the context. Lupton (1998) emphasizes that this distinction has a significant degree of overlap, but for the purposes of this chapter the social framework will receive the most emphasis. In particular, drawing on the mainly social approach to emotion which sees social reality as made up of many layers; layers which include the uniqueness of every person: their personality and life history, the context in which they work, and the people they work with. In leadership such layers are woven together, and given their meaning, by the affective (feeling) aspects of social reality.

Emotion and leadership

The concept of emotion is strongly linked to the aspects of leadership covered in earlier chapters in this book, giving us new insights into the practice of leadership and management. My particular view is that a better understanding of both concepts: emotion and leadership can enhance leaders' knowledge both of themselves and others. Ogawa and Bossert (1997: 19) suggest that: 'leadership flows through the network of roles that comprise organizations ... with different roles having access to different levels and types of resources'. Leaders help to create the conditions in which people will want to work to the optimum levels of their energy, interest and commitment (Whitaker 1997). Thus, this chapter focuses on extending knowledge of the affective domain, that is the part played by emotions in our lives, for those who practise or study leadership in education and elsewhere.

In terms of social reality, many practitioners in all kinds of organizations know of the concept of emotional intelligence, which will be considered later in this chapter. But there is more to emotion and leadership than this one aspect, however useful it may be. Law and Glover (2000: 263) suggest that educational leaders 'are expected to help others make sense of a complex world in which there is less predictability and more uncertainty – a major challenge which requires high-level skills, knowledge and understanding'. Whatever educational setting you work in, much of the work that is carried out has an affective aspect – engaging with the hearts and minds of young people and many different groups of people in the wider community context. It may be particularly important for leaders in diverse educational or other settings to be aware of all facets of relationships and how adults work, socialize and learn together given the sensitivities that exist around some areas of diversity. Leaders need to be awake to the fact that emotions are particularly engaged when we are dealing with such sensitive topics. For example Chugh and Brief (2008) talk about the emotion attached to talking openly about racial issues:

> When the conversations go sour, people's feelings get hurt. People are often misheard, misunderstood, and misread. There is usually a group that finds the conversation unnecessary while at the same time, another group that finds the conversation insufficient. And, somehow, everyone involved ends up feeling falsely accused of something.
>
> (Chugh and Brief 2008: 5)

There is further potential for misunderstanding in the work situation when there are differing cultural expectations about how emotions may be revealed and expressed. There are cultural differences in the extent to which people are likely to express their feelings, and the extent to which the expression of feelings is acceptable in the world of work. For example: 'there is a tendency for those with norms of emotional neutrality to dismiss anger, delight or intensity in the workplace as "unprofessional"' (Trompenaars and Hampden-Turner 1997: 72).

Leadership is a social function of the organization and the emotional resources available in an organization sustain all the people who work there. In other words, leadership is contained both in personal roles, such as 'Director of Children and Young People's Services' in England, and as a function within a social setting (in the example, that would include not only the local authority staff in offices, but also all the educational and social care staff in their particular settings). From my research, I would argue that leadership is reliant both on the personal emotional qualities of leaders, while being at the same time a quality of the social relationships of the contexts within which they work. The affective life of the organization is more than personal emotional knowledge, as leaders are sustained or defeated by the social relationships that they nurture. It is at the organizational level that the impact of emotion may be felt, and it is at the organizational level that many research studies have been carried out.

Defining emotion

The culture of an organization is created and sustained at least partly by the emotions of the participants, and that is why it is important that those in leadership roles learn more about their own and others' emotions. Even the very act of defining emotion may help leaders and can be seen as an aspect of the development of critical consciousness (see Chapter 1). For when we consider emotions, we often think of conscious displays of emotion, such as someone becoming angry. We may also think of unconscious or conscious feelings where what is going on inside is not visible outwardly, such as feeling angry but not displaying this to others. The whole area of leadership is concerned with how affect is woven into our lives without us necessarily being conscious of it most of the time. Emotion can be used to describe both this outward visible manifestation, and the feelings which we cannot see, but exist within the mind of the person concerned. Leaders need to explore how these aspects are interconnected. Thus, affective concerns are connected to areas such as values, principles and judgements (see Chapter 2); those very concepts that lend emotional colour, passion and individual purpose to leadership.

In this chapter I will concentrate on approaches to emotion which have a social aspect. The importance of the social perspective is that it draws on insights which have immediate practical applications for leaders, both in their own role, and in membership of other groups.

Reflection

How do you make judgements about a person's emotional state? What are you looking for? Bear this in mind as you consider the scenario.

The following scenario of a young female primary school deputy head teacher is drawn from my research. It highlights the complexity of the social aspects of leadership and emotion.

Scenario: Lack of emotional leadership in a small English school

Beth is a young woman who had just been appointed as deputy head teacher in a small junior school in England with eight full-time teaching members of staff, including herself. The school also had a new non-teaching head, three teaching assistants and several part-time teachers, one of whom, Harry, happened to be the previous head teacher. The catchment area was mixed, with private and social housing. Beth had previously worked for eight years in an outstanding school in a neighbouring local authority.

One of the other teachers, Joanne, had also applied for the deputy headship and was a highly popular, experienced member of the staff with expertise in special needs and literacy. Most of the staff deferred to her knowledge of children with difficulties. Martin, the head teacher, was a quiet organized person who seemed to enjoy the administrative side of his role. Harry, the former head, now worked part-time with Joanne to support the children with special needs. Except for Beth, they all had at least ten years' experience of teaching, and significantly more in Harry's case. Two members of staff had been in the school twenty-five years.

It soon became obvious to Beth that Joanne was very upset about not being offered the deputy post, and that she thought that Beth was young and inexperienced. Although outwardly she seemed pleasant, Beth noticed awkward silences when she came into the staff room, as if Joanne might have been discussing her, and one member of staff did actually comment that she thought Joanne was behaving unprofessionally.

Things came to a head in Beth's second year in post when there was a child in her class with severe problems in reading and behaviour, and Beth felt that she needed some specialist help. As Joanne was the special needs coordinator in the school, Beth asked if she could meet with her to discuss the child's needs. When they met, Joanne asked for details of the case and looked at the child's work. She then got up, looked at Beth and said, 'If you don't know how to handle this, then you shouldn't be in your position', and walked out. Beth described herself as feeling emotional: 'amazed and upset all at the same time'.

Coming from a very supportive, well-led school, Beth found the culture of her present school difficult to understand. Martin hardly ever came into the staff room (which was next to his office). Beth felt that the rest of the staff saw Joanne and Harry (the previous head and now a part-time teacher) as the people who could keep the school as it was, and that Martin and Beth were seen as incomers who might wish to change things.

Beth told Martin that she felt Joanne's behaviour to her was inexcusable and he agreed. He said it was not his role to talk to her, but that Beth should work out ways to work with her in order that she was happy. Beth did not feel that this was a satisfactory answer, but at the time was feeling so upset that she had no further discussion about it.

The aftermath

Two things then happened. Being a small divided school, both views of what had happened between Beth and Joanne got around staff. Harry, who had been a great supporter of Joanne, became more helpful towards Beth. Martin decided that the school needed another senior appointment to give Beth support and that he would offer it to another member of staff who shared his philosophy of education. He said he would tell Joanne personally about this, and when this meeting took place, the staff could hear her crying and shouting at him from the staff room next door. It later emerged that Martin had surprisingly offered her the post, 'to calm her down'. This was not helpful to Beth, or her position in the school!

Other members of staff began to realize that Joanne's behaviour was not conducive either to good staff relationships, or teaching and learning in the school. Joanne took a post with the behaviour support team in another area. Morale improved, but Martin did not change and continued to ignore emotional aspects of what was going on in the school. In the end, Beth too moved to another school in her original local authority as she found the work just too draining.

Reflection from Beth

My resolution was to leave for another job. At the time, I felt I just did not have the energy to stay, and this was compounded by a long commute to work. I could see that Martin was not going to change, and I felt that, despite things improving, my long-term health might suffer if I were to carry on teaching there. I suppose it was all I felt I could do at the time, but it did teach me the importance of leaders handling emotional situations. In the short term, it made me less trusting, but in the longer term, it has shown me that your own emotions are bound up with those of others in ways that can be very demanding. At the time it made me question all that I believed about people, and the intense emotions of other participants only served to make my own feelings more difficult to handle.

In order to reflect on this scenario, there are several perspectives that can help. One of these is the concept of emotional labour.

Emotional labour

Hochschild (1983) introduced the concept of emotional labour, where emotion can be viewed as a process that requires continuous conscious management within the work context. Hochschild viewed an individual's emotional state as being shaped by their position in the social system and in the power relations within that system, and was concerned to bring to the attention of researchers how emotion could be used for commercial ends, or what Hochschild called *'the managed heart'*. In order to conceptualize emotional labour, she drew upon her research on the role of emotion management in the life of flight attendants, and explored the tensions that build up when an individual has to give a particular performance as part of their job. She noted that female airline stewards for Delta had to make passengers feel welcome onboard, and were constantly exhorted to smile. From this extended research Hochschild (1983) devised the term 'emotional labour', where workers may be required to simulate or suppress feelings in themselves. For example the job of flight attendant requires them to maintain a specific outward appearance (smiles), which produces the required emotional state, in others (happy passengers). This can then be applied to other social transactions. She wrote:

> I use the term emotional labor to mean the management of feeling to create a publicly observable facial and bodily display; emotional labor is sold for a wage and therefore has exchange value.
>
> (Hochschild 1983: 7)

Hochschild stated that emotional labour operates through feeling rules. Feeling rules are those that are deemed to be appropriate to the social settings, such as happy when with good friends, sad at funerals, and so on. Hochschild argues that the individual's management of the feelings occurs through what Hochschild called surface and deep acting. Surface acting only requires the outward appearance (usually of a positive emotion such as happiness) and it does nothing to resolve tensions brought about by acting in a way that is different to how the individual actually feels. Deep acting is different in that deep acting involves 'visualizing a substantial portion of reality in a different way' (Hochschild 1983: 121). In other words, deep acting requires a different way of looking at a situation. It may mean that a leader has to visualize and change an organizational situation so that social reality becomes more in tune with, for example, their own values, and the deep acting may require a change of their internal emotion state or feelings. To do this, they need support from others both within and outside the organization if they are to sustain such deep acting over a long period. This was something that Joanne, the young deputy and her head teacher in the scenario had not considered. It seemed that none of the individuals in the scenario was successfully undertaking emotional labour. Joanne was barely able to contain her feelings about Beth even before their meeting about the child with problems. Those concerned were not practising deep acting or even surface acting. It is also possible that emotional labour was being seen as something undertaken by women rather than men. The head teacher (a man) distanced himself from the emotions of the (mainly women) around him and expected them to deal with emotional issues themselves.

Emotional labour provides one insight into the deputy's situation. When you take up a leadership role, you work both with expressed emotion and the unknown inner feelings of others. Was there anything the deputy in the scenario could have foreseen in terms of the emotion of the situation? How could she have identified difficulties? She was relatively inexperienced, having worked in only one well-led school prior to her appointment. She does not appear to have exercised empathy in establishing relationships with her new colleagues. However, her head teacher was disengaged from the emotional issues among his staff and seemed to have no insights into how to resolve the emotional turmoil around him.

One other area of research into emotion which is pertinent to the scenario is how people regulate their emotions so as to keep them in balance. There are many ways of looking at this but Gross and John (2002: 299) suggest that we can learn by experience which responses are more likely to give the best result in any given situation. The deputy, who was relatively young, was lacking in this experience of how to manage difficult emotions.

Reflection

Are you aware of situations where you are undertaking emotional labour in your professional role?

In this chapter, we are mainly looking at emotion from a social perspective but it has been investigated extensively from the psychological perspective, and the following sections briefly outline some of these ideas. In this perspective the view is that emotions are basically inherent, and it is important to recognize that it is against this psychological backcloth that the social world is constructed.

The psychological approach

In terms of the psychological literature, a great deal of the emotion management undertaken by people in public service organizations is response focused – that is managing the public perception of their emotion while a situation is occurring. In schools for example there is an expectation that the head teacher is in control of the situation. This has obvious links to the concept of emotional labour, where the leader may be practising surface or deep acting in carrying out their role.

An important concept within the psychological approach is that of cognitive appraisal, where a person is faced with events, appraises them, and decides how best to handle them. Here the term 'appraisal' is used in a general sense, not in the specialized sense of appraisal as part of performance review. Leaders may find a brief explanation of some of the background information on how and why this occurs valuable in their own decision-making and that of others. The work of Lazarus (1991) is of particular relevance here. Lazarus argued that emotions are elicited by significant events. According to Lazarus (1991), a primary appraisal of an event has three features:

- *Goal relevance:* emotion occurs only if an event is relevant to a concern or a goal.
- *Goal congruence or incongruence:* this causes positive emotions to occur when moving towards a goal, moving away from a goal causes negative emotions.
- *Ego involvement:* how much involvement someone has in the event, encompassing the value the person puts on the event.

These three features are interesting to consider in the light of the scenario. For Joanne, the older teacher, Beth's appointment was an example of goal relevance bringing about negative emotion because of goal incongruence. Her ego involvement was high as she really wanted the role that was given to Beth. Ego involvement could be said to be of primary importance. Emotion can be suppressed or acted upon, depending often on the person's history and experience of similar events. Or as Solomon (2000) puts it:

> What remains at the core of all theories however is awareness that all emotions presuppose or have as their preconditions certain sorts of cognitions – an awareness of danger in fear, recognition of an offence in anger, appreciation of someone or something lovable in love.
>
> (Solomon 2000: 11)

Haviland-Jones and Kahlbaugh (2004) suggest that emotions and thoughts are the things that are most real to people at any given moment, and that one of the functions of emotion is to glue together chunks of experience to provide meaning. It could be argued that one of the leaders' functions is to help provide that framework of meaning (Fineman 2003).

Another related aspect to emotion which has been given little attention in educational leadership is that of temperament. Research (Caspi et al. 1987, 1988) indicates that there are patterns of childhood emotionality that people carry with them into adulthood. In their follow-up work (30 years later) of adults who had been ill-tempered at age eight, they discovered that some patterns were relatively enduring, if gendered. For example men who were assessed as ill-tempered as children were less likely to stay on at school, and more likely to move jobs. Women who were assessed as ill-tempered were more affected in their home life, having more frequent divorces than women who were assessed as even-tempered at age eight. You may find the view of Saarni (2000), a developmental psychologist, helpful:

> Temperament provides some degree of response style consistency over time and across situations, whereas specific emotional reactions yield the variability that comes from the influence of specific contexts, specific appraisals, specific social transactions, and the unique meaning systems that are applied to make sense of emotional experience.
>
> (Saarni 2000: 312)

In this chapter we will not be covering the theoretical dilemmas within developmental psychology, such as whether emotional development is most influenced by temperament or context (the nature versus nurture debate), but you may wish to explore its leadership potential further. Culture and context are the setting for your individual history, your life so far, and how you assume the identity of an educational leader. This is part of the social construction of reality (Berger and Luckmann 1991), and the culture of the organization. The way that you conceptualize your own leadership will have an impact on the way that you practise that leadership.

Emotional intelligence

Emotional intelligence was originally a psychological concept, but over time, it has been developed into something that is more akin to a competency approach to emotion, items that can be measured in a check list. It can be argued that the architects of emotional intelligence are the team of Salovey and Mayer. Their original work, and the emphasis within it, was concerned with a discrete set of conceptually related mental processes that involve emotional information. They view these key processes as a way of approaching what they called 'life tasks', with what they call emotional intelligence (Salovey and Mayer 1990, 2001). This concept was later popularized by Goleman (1995, 1998). These four processes are:

- Appraisal and expression of emotion (self and others)
- Regulation of emotion
- Utilization of emotion
- Emotion's facilitation of thinking.

The processes within the Goleman (1995) version of emotional intelligence are:

- *Self-awareness:* the ability to understand your own emotions
- *Self-management:* the ability to control and adapt your own emotions, as in emotional labour
- *Social awareness:* the ability to correctly divine and respond to others
- *Relationship management:* the ability to manage others and their emotions in a group.

This research on emotion struck a chord with those concerned with leadership, perhaps because of the emphasis on the intra-personal and interpersonal (inherent and social), and the fact that these emotional processes were related to life skills. Salovey et al. (2000) considered it important that individuals were able to apply these processes to emotional content in social situations, assessing their own feelings, and those of others, accurately. These processes appear to have direct application to leadership, and this has been further developed by Goleman (1995). Salovey et al. (2000) also suggested that emotion helps the processing of information as well as developing multiple options in any given situation. Leadership demands a high level of emotional reasoning.

It may be that intra-personal skills will be enhanced through reflection and the critical consciousness discussed in Chapter 1. Leaders can develop such knowledge over time in relationships as well as becoming more able to consciously reflect on their own emotional state at any one time. The deputy head in the scenario was, in a sense, doing this as she told the story of the events that happened to her. You may like to consider how aspects of emotional intelligence are pertinent to the main 'players' in the scenario. It would seem that they were not being emotionally intelligent in any of the four ways outlined above. In particular, Martin the head teacher showed an absence of social awareness and relationship management.

Salovey et al. (2000) state:

> We believe that emotional competencies are fundamental to so-
> cial intelligence. This is because social problems and situations
> are laden with affective information. Moreover, emotional com-
> petences apply not only to social experiences but to experiences
> within the individual.
>
> (Salovey et al. 2000: 504)

Goleman (1995) developed these ideas into his competence framework,
which has become so popular. Fineman (2000: 102) notes that it has always been known that certain work relationships require emotional skills,
but what Goleman has succeeded in doing is linking such competences
explicitly to success. Leading a team is a role that requires emotional skill,
and the climate has been right for emotional intelligence to take its place
among other leadership strategies perhaps because of the emphasis on
competencies, targets and league tables. As leadership becomes more difficult to sustain, wider social trends, such as a willingness to discuss stress
in organizations, mean that emotional intelligence has been seen as a
possible solution to a problem of recruitment and sustainability. Perhaps
the popularity of emotional intelligence is due, at least partially, to the
fact that it reminds leaders what they probably already knew; that emotion and thinking do work together, and that there has perhaps been too
much emphasis on the rational and not enough on the power of emotion and feeling. Emotional intelligence's popularity could also be because
rational discussion of emotional competences is emotionally safe, and
does not necessarily require or suggest a change in your inner emotional
state.

Emotional context

Emotional labour and emotional intelligence are two concepts from research that seem to apply particularly well to leadership in education.
Emotion, then, is not only part of the individual but also part of the social aspect of the organization. This is because organizational emotion is
embodied in the leader and those who are led. It is part of their outward
display and their inner feeling: the inherent and socially constructed aspects of emotion working together. Both of these aspects make up the
emotional context of organizations.

An idea which many leaders in education may find compelling is that
of the wounded leader. The scenario is an example of a wound. Beth is
the leader who is wounded as a result of the unmanaged and unrecog-
nized negative emotions in the school. Arguing that all leaders will have

difficult emotional experiences which leave wounds, Ackerman and Maslin-Ostrowski (2004) state:

> The wound thus can serve as a call to examine the foundation of one's leadership. Like illness, a leadership wound brings not only difficulty and danger but also awareness and opportunity. For some of the leaders we met who had sacrificed their identity and integrity in the name of leadership, the wound was a wake-up call to their real self. They found the means – some call it courage – to shed inauthentic ways of being and became truer to themselves, more whole again. For others, the change was not about being different, but finding new meaning in what they were already doing. Some leaders used the moment to resist becoming anything else, hoping to move forward into the future unaltered. Some were changed spontaneously and unthinkingly from within or without. Still others were changed deliberately and consciously, never easily, never for sure, and only with effort, insight, and courage. The experience of leadership suffering – of the wound – is itself a defining characteristic of leaders and leadership.
>
> (Ackerman and Maslin-Ostrowski 2004: 13–14)

Beginning to understand how leadership emerges from the social setting and interacts with someone's inner world, in this case through wounding, may have a profound impact, because leadership is an important and essential component that helps to emotionally sustain organizations.

If wounding is a defining characteristic of leaders, particularly in the way that it helps them learn more about themselves as leaders, then it would seem right to argue that this experience is not only essential, but also that it cannot be rationalized out of leaders' experiences. The experience of wounding is commonplace and it serves to highlight the importance of emotion in leadership for sustainability in leadership over time.

Whitaker (1997: 127) used the concept of 'life-enhancing leadership' and notes in the primary school context that:

> It is through the countless interpersonal transactions of the school day that people's lives are changed, organizational improvements are made, dreams are realized and needs are met. We need more understanding of those snatched moments in corridors. ... Life-centred leadership is essentially a catalytic process, helping others to bring about changes in themselves.
>
> (Whitaker 1997: 140)

He suggests that people's knowledge of their own emotional self enables them to visualize how they want others to relate to each other within the school (staff, parents and children), within an emotional coherent context. As a leader, the need to deepen self-knowledge of one's self emotionally relates to such outward expressions of feelings, at the same time the self-knowledge generates a powerful emotional context for people working within an educational organization.

Concluding thoughts

Having considered some theoretical aspects of emotion and leadership, several thoughts occur in relation to the scenario:

- The leader forms and makes manifest an emotional context within which the other important narrative, education, is carried out. In this case, Martin, for whatever reason, was distant emotionally, and found outward displays of emotionality hard to handle. He was not able to help his deputy with this aspect of leadership.
- The deputy had come from a school that was very successful. We could argue that one of the reasons her new school was less successful was because neither the deputy nor the head were able to visualize how they want others in the organization to relate to each other, and help them to do so. They were unable to sustain an emotionally coherent context.
- The main 'players' concerned with events in the school were all wounded in one way or another, but were not able to move forward. The deputy was wounded as a leader.
- Emotional labour was not a feature of the leadership of the school. It is possible that the deputy may have been surface acting before her meeting with Joanne as she ignored signs of friction, but deep acting to resolve the situation would have been difficult without the leadership of the head.

There are connections between emotion in leadership and all the areas covered in this book. The values that underpin leadership are linked to emotions, and just to take one specific area, there are obvious connections between emotions and their management and the skills discussed in the chapter on communication. Emotion and leadership provides a rich and complex area to explore and will provide educational leaders with further insights to inform the day to day practice of leading.

Summary

In this chapter we have mainly taken a view of emotions as socially constructed although recognizing the psychological approach to emotion.

The scenario indicates the importance of emotions within an organizational culture and the need for leaders to be emotionally literate. With relevance to educational leadership, particular attention was paid to the concepts of emotional intelligence, emotional labour and the wounded leader.

Further reading

More examples of such leadership and emotion scenarios can be found in: Crawford, M. (2009) *Getting to the Heart of Leadership: Emotion and the Educational Leader*. London: Sage.

Other useful references for more on the links between emotions and leadership are: Fineman, S. (ed.) (2000) *Emotion in Organisations*. London: Sage.

Harris, B. (2007) *Supporting the Emotional Work of School Leaders*. London: Sage.

Loader, D. (1997) *The Inner Principal*. London: Falmer.

11 Personal and institutional development

The learning community

In this final chapter we look at the way in which the individuals within an organization and the organization itself can continue to 'grow' so that the relationship between the school, college or other organization and the environment within which it works is symbiotic and dynamic. For this to occur, the organization has to continue to learn at all levels. This implies engaging with the management of change as the learning community is a changing community with adaptations being made in the light of changed professional knowledge, socio-economic structures and cultural expectations. The chapter starts with an overview of learning opportunities and then moves on to consider the theory on how adults learn. The scenario focuses on how staff can learn together to bring about institutional improvement and the final section focuses on three important ways in which individuals can develop their professional skills, through mentoring, coaching and facilitating.

When teachers are part of a learning community they will adapt to, and influence, the change which is all around them. We are concerned with enhancing the readiness of teachers and others in education to undertake further development. This can be at two levels – the personal, whereby one or more staff develop specific skills and understanding (e.g. in the integration of new technology into teaching and learning), and the institutional, offering development objectives for the institution as a whole. The relationship between the two is shown in part of the national guidelines for head teachers in Wales.

> Leading learning and teaching: The head teacher, working with the staff and governors, creates the conditions and structures to support effective learning and teaching for all. Head teachers have a direct responsibility for the quality of learning and teaching and for pupils' achievement. This implies setting high expectations and monitoring and evaluating the effectiveness of learning outcomes.
>
> (National Assembly of Wales 2005: 3)

One example of staff support for the benefit of the teaching and learning in the school can be seen in England, where the National College for Leadership in Schools and Children's Services is trying to offer a number of strategies to help people at every stage of their career. The National College has encouraged local authorities, the equivalent of school boards, to allow experienced staff moving towards retirement to work part-time so that they continue to provide examples of effective teaching and offer support to younger members of staff who will replace them in two or three years' time. The human resources are thus managed to promote pupil achievement within a learning community (Bush et al. 2008).

There are many activities, both formal and informal, that promote the learning and professional development of staff that go well beyond traditional courses and workshops, and Earley (2005) offers an overview of some activities now in use. These are classified as: observing good practitioners either in the classroom or in meetings; extending professional experience through school-based training; personal profile development; networking and team teaching; and working with pupils through corporate learning activities, supported e-learning and mentoring. Indeed, Earley (2005) notes: 'Research suggests that "on the job" experiences are seen as more significant than "off the job" experiences, although there is a clear need for both' (Earley 2005: 238). In the scenario later in this chapter, the whole school is involved in action research, a particularly effective type of individual and institutional development. The combination of well-managed informal and formal opportunities can create vibrancy and excitement within the organization. The informal activities that affect the culture of the organization include applying critical thinking to work, or holding what Brookfield (1987) calls 'learning conversations'. Gold (2004) points out that:

> It is not always necessary to spend a great deal of money and time to encourage continuous professional development. An educative school which pays attention to learning and teaching for everyone within the school community buzzes with discussions and thought-provoking arguments, as well as planned formal learning opportunities.
>
> (Gold 2004: 33)

Opportunities for learning can be great motivators. Earlier in the book we have looked at the development of delegation and the importance of teams in educational organizations. As leadership becomes more distributed more teachers have to adopt leadership roles and promote school effectiveness through their own endeavours. Grant (2006) suggests three levels of approach to organizational learning with practices developing from within the classroom, through the greater development of working relationships with other colleagues, to involvement in whole school issues such as vision and policy development. For this to evolve the starting point has to be with individual learning – just what is the best approach to personal and organizational professional development?

The pattern of adult learning

Tusting and Barton (2006) offer a summary of learning approaches and as we reflect on our own learning we can see how we react in particular situations. This will be affected by our own experience, cultural background and relationship to our communities – all aspects of our personal and professional environment already considered in Chapter 1 on diversity. Learning approaches may differ as follows:

- Behaviourist research shows how we are helped to attain changed performance through behaviour change. This can be trained by breaking down complex chains of behaviour into simpler steps and rewarding learners when they perform each step. Gradually learners approximate more and more closely to the desired behaviour. However, these approaches cannot address the non-material aspects of learning and understanding that are at the heart of learning.
- A cognitive perspective shows that behaviour does not necessarily correlate with understanding, and that we need to find ways to build on people's existing knowledge to help them make sense of new information. Cognitive constructivism brings to light the learner's active role in this process, and the need to support learners in making their own meanings and connections.
- Developmental theories add the understanding that people pass through different stages in their lives, in which they take on different social and cultural roles and responsibilities. Provision needs to take account of this and find ways to understand and respond to the practices and problems people engage with in their lives outside the classroom. It is important to resist inappropriate models of adult development, particularly those that assume there is a single developmental path and end-point towards which we should all be aiming.

(Tusting and Barton 2006: 43–44)

As we saw in Chapters 5 and 7 on motivation and teams, we have to recognize that as individuals we have differing motivators when faced with professional development at either a personal or organizational level.

Tusting and Barton (2006) also draw the following inferences from their review of the literature:

1. Adults have their own motivations for learning building on their existing knowledge and experience.
2. Adults have a drive towards self-direction and towards becoming autonomous learners.
3. Adults have the ability to learn about their own learning processes, and can benefit from discussion and reflection on this.
4. Learning is a characteristic of all real-life activities, in which people take on different roles and participate in different ways.
5. Reflective learning is generated when people encounter problems and issues in their real lives and think about ways of resolving them.
6. A great deal of learning is incidental and idiosyncratically related to the learner: it cannot be planned in advance.
7. Reflective learning enables people to reorganize experience and 'see' situations in new ways.

(Tusting and Barton 2006: 45–46)

The work situation offers opportunities for learning from experience and can help individuals understand how they construct knowledge. As a result, they are able to respond with increasing awareness to the complexities of adult lives, such as conflicts between their values and their current life choices. But we have to recall the balance between individual and institutional needs.

One of the aspects of personal and school or college development is that it is not always possible to ascertain the focus of activity. For example, often the phrase 'leadership development' is used to mean training for headship or senior management roles but this implies training for hierarchical situations. In their review of the literature, Muijs and Harris (2003) suggest that providing opportunities for teachers to become involved in aspects of leadership at all levels opens the way to a new professionalism breaking away from hierarchical control structures to a more creative way of working with differing assumptions of status and power structures. However, they see the need for the brokering and mediating of relationships between colleagues, for some surrender of power by senior leaders who should be imbued with the collaborative philosophy, and for a transformation of organizations into professional learning communities.

Leading or managing teaching and learning therefore involves teachers at all levels of school or college organization. While there is a global trend towards devolved, or institutionally based, management, schools are increasingly subject to local or national guidance and with this are made to be accountable through published results, inspections and stakeholder involvement. Therefore the teacher is increasingly free to teach as he or she believes to be most effective but also increasingly constrained to produce results however these may be defined.

Reflection

After reading this section consider a recent learning experience in the light of the theory outlined – do you agree or disagree with the picture we have given of adult learning? Does leadership learning differ from organizational or professional learning?

Approaches to learning

You may or may not agree that the ultimate purpose of all institutional development in education is the enhancement of teaching and learning, but that is why professional development is made available to teachers. Some teachers may be too dependent upon transmissive approaches to teaching and learning, for themselves and their students, and judge the effectiveness of developmental activity only in terms of what they have been told. Transmissive approaches can dominate because, among other things:

- They fit existing frameworks, replicating teachers' own experience.
- They fit well with accountability systems based on outputs.
- They present fewer organizational problems because they are hierarchichal in nature.
- They are 'tidier' than more creative approaches.

By contrast experiential learning is more difficult to manage, requires much more understanding of learning methods, is more difficult to assess and frequently offers challenges to those who are hoping to convince others. For example, experiential learning as in the Kolb (1984) learning cycle identifies stages where, we make sense of a concrete experience by reflecting on it and conceptualizing it, then working or experimenting with the conceptualization. These stages can be seen in the application of theory to practice. Argyris and Schön (1981) developed this further to talk about single and double loop learning. In single loop learning changes are made as a result of reflection when something does not work out well. In double loop learning we might go further to question or 'problematize' the assumptions underlying the activity.

Individuals may show a preference in their learning for one or more of the four stages in the Kolb cycle, and Honey and Mumford (1988) have built on the theory to identify four learning styles:

- *Activists:* 'hands-on' learners who prefer to have a go and learn through trial and error.
- *Reflectors:* 'tell me' learners who prefer to be thoroughly briefed before proceeding.
- *Theorists:* 'convince me' learners who want reassurance that a project makes sense.
- *Pragmatists:* 'show me' learners who want a demonstration from an acknowledged expert.

(based on Honey 2009)

These styles are summarized by Law and Glover (2000: 170) as learning by 'feeling, watching, thinking or doing'.

As a result institutional development requires attention to what Gardner (1983) described as multiple intelligences. It is easy to suggest that ideas can be represented in a variety of ways, such as linguistic, kinaesthetic or interpersonal, but less easy to apply these to meet the needs of the teams being asked to look at institutional change. If these are taken into account by leaders then colleagues gain from understanding their own strengths and needs and recognize that in working with others a variety of approaches may be beneficial.

Scenario: Helping a school move forward in New Zealand

Carol Cardno has worked extensively in professional development in New Zealand and has outlined the progress of the staff of one junior school as they came to understand each other better while she acted as a mentor and consultant. Success depended upon developing an openness between and across layers of staff within the school. With Carol's permission we are using some material from her article (Cardno 2006) summarizing the developments. While her emphasis is on the way in which effective professional growth can be achieved we are, in a sense, sitting on her shoulder to see the role played by helping participants to recognize and build on opportunities for development.

The context

Within self-governing primary schools in New Zealand a hierarchy of responsibility has developed with senior management teams of principal assisted by either deputy or associate principals developing and directing policies for school leadership and management. At a lower level are 'syndicates' or groups of teachers led by middle managers responsible for teaching and learning. Within these syndicates for each of three age-related teaching teams there are also curriculum leaders who then meet with those teaching their subject in curriculum meetings. The potential for misunderstanding within such a system is considerable and the principal of the case study school under review felt that enhanced involvement of all staff should grow from some understanding of roles. This would be the starting point for broader review and developmental planning.

The overwhelming question of the effectiveness of role and responsibility structures puts people under some threat because the status quo is being challenged. Will the staff understand the principal's intention; how will they represent what they are thinking to each other at each management layer level; how will teachers in leadership positions explain what is behind the thinking to other members of staff? All this stems from the principal's desire for effective development but so much depends upon the way in which this is managed at individual and group or school levels.

Approaches

The principal worked with the staff of a higher education college to develop an approach which would involve all staff from the beginning of an action research programme. By action research was meant an opportunity for participants to identify an issue requiring attention and then following a research discipline to investigate, explain, reflect upon and make recommendations for development. To start this process a full day facilitation meeting was arranged for the senior management team (SMT), the associate principals and the curriculum leaders (nine people in all) at the start of a school year.

The aim of the project, to investigate the role of curriculum teams and their leadership, was offered as the starting point. However, by the end of this first day the group was in agreement regarding some of the dimensions of the problem, which they summarized as follows:

- workloads
- developing leaders
- need to clarify the status quo by examining documents and expectations
- need to examine the literature on curriculum leadership
- need for SMT to jointly own issues related to the problem

- recognition that something is not quite right with curriculum leadership:
    - role of curriculum leaders needs investigating
    - role and responsibilities of curriculum teams needs clarification
    - role and responsibilities of associate principals in relation to curriculum
    - leadership need clarification.

(Cardno 2006: 460)

From the point of view of development strategy the first day had yielded real benefits.

1. There was an understanding of the project and how to take it forward by those most involved.
2. There was understanding and agreement that although there might be extra work for all involved there would be gains in the long run.
3. There was agreement on what was under the spotlight so that everyone could see that there was a clear idea of 'what was up for change'.

It seems that in this work the team had become more open, flexible in their working and ready to listen to others. This was seen in their report on the current function of curriculum teams where they were:

- giving all staff the opportunity to participate in curriculum resource decision-making in at least one curriculum area
- providing a form of professional development to 'grow leaders' who were passionate about a curriculum area
- reducing the work of the SMT by delegating it formally to other middle managers.

We have outlined only the start of the process. Once developmental possibilities were identified and understood, there was professional growth and a move towards shared status. Ideas had been developed, implemented and evaluated without perceived threats to any member of staff and all staff then wanted to be involved. The principal was seen as acting in a collegial manner; the SMT gained from working in this way when other aspects of policy were under review; there was open discussion of ideas within the school community; and the changes were evaluated as contributing to enhanced effectiveness. For the principal the gains were considerable because the staff were more ready to take on additional curriculum responsibilities and to share ideas for further development . . . and it all involved open communication and the opportunity for enhanced understanding.

> ## Reflection
>
> What elements of this case study do you recognize as occurring or not occurring within your working environment? Perhaps you can outline a similar programme that might be advantageous in your school or college – what would be your statement of objectives to secure the greatest change?

Lesson observation and implementing policies

To understand both progress and problems in organizational development it is sometimes necessary for all teachers to be open to being observed at work either by colleagues, peers or superiors. This may mean as part of meetings, or within the classroom or in interaction with individuals or groups. However, this requires a culture of sufficient openness to have been developed, otherwise there may be problems for those who feel in any way marginalized within the school or college. If peer or superior observation against agreed criteria is developed as part of the life of the school, this marginalization will be minimized. Once colleagues are prepared to share their experiences the focus will move from teachers feeling that they are the subject of observation to mutual understanding of what needs to be further researched. When this has been undertaken a strategy of supported development either through co-working, facilitation or mentoring becomes possible at individual or group level.

As you think about the scenario above, and possibly have a look at the full article, you will realize that the head teacher was concerned to secure a positive development within the school. This involves elements of enhanced communications, an understanding of the management of change, and personal and group professional development. But where does the impact of development occur? Essentially it is within teaching and learning. O'Sullivan (2006) stresses that educational quality can be improved only if there is systematic observation of what is happening there. This may be to remedy what is not taking place, to ensure competence, to add quality and value to the learning process and to understand more of the context within which teaching and learning takes place. All that happens in the classroom contributes to evidence under all these headings but requires effective observation which includes recording, analysing and reflecting on interrelationships, interactions and outcomes. O'Sullivan (2006) suggests that the process of observation needs sharpening if appropriate support is to be developed. This requires some assessment of the criteria against which classroom observation takes place. The author feels that:

> classroom-based methods, including lesson observations, learner interviews, and teacher interviews, are critical methods in the effective measurement of quality in teaching and learning. They provide insights critical to assessing and improving quality, which are otherwise inaccessible.
>
> (O'Sullivan 2006: 253)

However, the outcomes of such observations are of value only if they are the basis of further training and development.

Making a difference: mentoring, coaching and facilitating

As we have seen there can be synergy in individual and institutional development. Within a learning community, individuals can be supported and challenged to improve their own professional skills and knowledge, benefiting the organization as a whole. Increasingly use is being made of three professional development techniques that help in making a difference for educators in changing situations – these are mentoring, coaching and facilitating. In a community such as that identified in our scenario, where there is clarity about the focus of development, these techniques will be most beneficial.

Mentoring

Mentoring is person centred, and there is increased awareness of the need to match mentor and mentee, to ensure that mentors are properly trained and that there is time, support and understanding through reflection on the process – rather more than getting the job done! Peer and engagement mentoring are comparatively new arrivals. Luck (2003) summarized this for the National College for School Leadership, noting that all the mentees and mentors could easily identify the very practical ways in which the experience of mentoring had helped to improve their skills and made them more effective. For example, in relation to developing ability to lead people to work towards common goals, those who were mentored said that mentoring by experienced colleagues had helped them to develop their expertise in interviewing new staff and motivating people. They had also learnt new skills such as challenging built-in assumptions, and even found that they were making better use of time. Some of these elements can be seen in the scenario in Chapter 9, when the mentor helps Jane develop

a more positive attitude to her work. Those who have been mentors recognize the benefits in reflecting on their own practice and developing greater objectivity as a result.

There has been considerable research into the effectiveness of mentoring. Mathews (2003) claims that mentoring, as a workplace learning approach, could be used to address the problems associated with the recruitment and attrition of academic staff and adds that mentoring roles may be diverse, including those of guide, teacher, adviser, friend, tutor, catalyst, coach, consultant, role model and advocate. For success there has to be careful match of mentor and mentee. Halai (2006), referring to practice in Pakistan, says that mentors working as 'expert-coach' create or reinforce status differentials in mentor-mentee relationships, and this can be counterproductive. Angelique et al. (2002) in a review of 'peer mentoring', an alternative to this traditional mentoring involving people of similar age and experience, note success where specific skills are being developed but there is often a need for someone to mentor by promoting reflection on skills, attitudes and behaviours.

For mentoring to be effective, Carroll (2005: 465) suggests that there needs to be a new approach within the meetings, bringing different elements together through an inquiry perspective as follows:

- *Restating:* repeating an idea to invite additional attention or concurrence.
- *Recycling:* reintroducing an idea from earlier in the session to position it in relation to a current observation.
- *Reconceptualizing:* developing or broadening an example into a more general idea.
- *Recontextualizing:* shifting the perspectives brought to bear on it.
- *Making a warranted inference:* to make an inference based on the previous speaker's comment and implicitly invite concurrence or disagreement.

There can be tensions within mentoring relationships. For example, Stead (2006) identifies tensions arising from feelings of exposure and vulnerability on the part of the mentee and raises issues of power and influence as mentors' controlling forces. Similar tensions are discussed in relation to mentoring and diversity in Chapter 1. While it is argued that successful mentoring requires trust and commitment, research evidence from human resource literature points to potential difficulties where structures inhibit open relationships. Work pressures may also mean that the mentee needs time from a mentor who, because of his or her responsibility, cannot respond. Stead (2006: 181) argues that novice leaders are not helped by mentoring because the pressures of the new context can detract from effective reflection.

In Chapter 1 the concept of reverse mentoring was introduced. This can be of value in raising consciousness of diversity issues, for example where the mentor may be younger or of different gender or ethnicity or sexual orientation. The mentor who is junior to the mentee is coached to develop skills so that he or she can give feedback to their mentee on developing their capacity as a diversity leadership role model. This offers a double benefit in development terms for the mentoring pair. The importance of diverse role models was also considered in Chapter 1, for example the existence of a black woman in a leadership position can offer a stimulus for others from minority backgrounds to aspire to senior posts (Carroll and Hannan 2000). The sensitivity of these issues may, however, require considerable one to one support.

Coaching

Coaching is a more specific form of adult learning, because it has specified objectives – usually to learn a set of competences in regard to a particular role. Bassett (2001) states that coaching differs from mentoring, as the stress is on skills development. This suggests that coaching is being conceptualized as training whereas mentoring is seen as a more reflective process. Bloom et al. (2005) make an important distinction between these development strategies. Mentors can relate to newcomers 'showing them the ropes' in any number of situations. A coach, on the other hand, provides continuing support that is safe and confidential and has as its goal the nurturing of significant personal, professional and institutional growth through a process that unfolds over time. A coach brings an outside perspective and has no stake in the status quo in an organization. Coaching is a professional practice; mentoring is often voluntary and informal (Bloom et al. 2005: 9–10) although it too can be formalized. Bloom et al. (2005) summarize coaching in the following way:

> Sometimes it is appropriate for a coach to teach, to use didactic methods in order to help a coachee to achieve a goal. Coaches typically use instructional strategies when they are focusing on a coachee's way of doing. For example, to help a coachee get into classrooms more often, a coach might provide an article on time management and work with the coachee to set up new office systems. The coach might shadow the coachee and suggest concrete changes in behaviour and process that would make it possible for the coachee to protect the time set aside for classroom observations. Each of these instructional steps would help the principal do a better job of getting into classrooms.
>
> Over time, we change who we are by changing what we do. However, instructional strategies have limitations. They may

encourage dependence rather than independence. They teach specific knowledge and skills but fall short when it comes to building fundamental capacity. Coaches can help coachees internalize learning and be transformed by it through facilitative strategies, strategies that are constructivist in nature. These support the coachee in learning new ways of being through observation, reflection, analysis, reinterpretation, and experimentation.

(Bloom et al. 2005: 96)

Recognizing this definition, Creasy and Patterson (2005) set out the principles and practicalities of supportive coaching for leadership in a workbook produced for the National College for School Leadership (NCSL) for English schools. They differentiate between types of coaching as follows:

- *Informal coaching:* conversations where a school leader or peer uses coaching principles in short informal conversations about an issue raised by a colleague. As well as supporting the development of thinking and practice, this can model professional learning dialogue.
- *Specialist coaching:* working with a colleague who has specialist knowledge, such as an advanced skills teacher (AST) or National Strategy consultant. By virtue of their experience and expertise, a specialist coach supports development in a specific area of practice, for instance in Assessment for Learning or classroom environment. In addition to specialist expertise, specialist coaches will have developed an understanding of coaching principles, skills and qualities whether as a superior or peer colleague.
- *Team coaching:* working as a department, for example on behaviour management, led by an external or expert coach with expertise in this area, expert coaching working with an expert coach to develop coaching skills, where expert coaches model and develop coaching skills across the school.
- *Expert coaching:* may form part of external training for coaching or be part of in-school development of coaching practice. Expert coaches will have, and develop in others, a clear understanding of the adult learning principles that underpin effective coaching in schools and high order coaching skills and qualities. They understand and focus upon the process of professional learning as well as supporting an individual's focus.
- *Pupil coaching:* promoting pupil-to-pupil coaching is a powerful learning process. Coaching that works in similar ways at all levels in the school provides a robust mechanism that reinforces its importance as a learning tool.

- *Self-coaching:* when reflecting on issues of professional concern, coaching principles and protocols can be usefully used to structure self-coaching.

(based on Creasy and Patterson 2005: 18)

As we have seen there is often a concern about the power relationships between the mentor and those being supported often because of the need to explore issues of a broader philosophical nature. Coaching may be more time limited and related to the acquisition of particular skills and so if there are breakdowns in relationships while there may be immediate loss alternative support can be found. Our final approach to professional development is concerned with facilitation: working alongside people where status structures are much less relevant.

Facilitating

The introduction of new technologies into educational organizations relies upon the training of teachers in both the management of the technology (competence and confidence) and its integration into teaching (pedagogy). Glover et al. (2007) show how many teachers need help in both areas because they are unsure of aspects of classroom management while they are learning to use electronic whiteboards to maximum teaching advantage. Our research group found that the successful introduction of new technology with a positive impact on pupil attainment relies heavily upon in-school support from a skilled and confident colleague who has both enthusiasm and the ability, and time, to help others as they develop new approaches and materials. They are facilitators helping others to gain what they have learnt.

It could be argued that we are dealing with semantics in differing between the terms used for supporting colleagues. However, Rigg and Richards (2005) argue that developmental support needs to be multifaceted (with elements of mentor, coach or facilitator according to the situation) and bilingual (practitioner and academic according to the focus). They claim that facilitating is a craft, with multiple moments of judgement, and choices to be made. There are also manifold opportunities for facilitators to learn from experience and, like their participants, to gain insights from experimentation and reflection. They add that, as facilitators are people too, they bring their own anxieties, impulses to control and responses to uncertainty, which influence the process of action learning as much as dynamics between the group participants (Rigg and Richards 2005: 202).

Mackeracher (2004: 206) identifies three basic strategies that typify many approaches to facilitating: directing, enabling and collaborating.

Each must be considered both as part of a continuum of facilitating behaviours and as unique by itself; each strategy has advantages and disadvantages. Good facilitators are able to use all three strategies in varying
combinations depending on the material, the learners, and the setting of
the learning activities.

There is an increasing tendency to move from directing and enabling
support to collaborative working, which is much more in tune with sharing the vision in an organization. In this situation co-learners are enabled
to grow individually and as members of a team, for example, through
community problem-solving, groups or work-related project teams (see
Chapter 7 on teams). This is most effective where the focus is defined by
the co-learners, and through processes, structures and directions negotiated and so resulting in a group consensus.

Reflection

What do you think are your three most significant personal professional
needs at present. Consider the applicability of the three approaches outlined above in relation to these needs. Are there some needs that cannot
be met in these ways?

A learning culture

A learning culture can only really exist where there is mutual understanding and collaboration. Earley (2005) states that:

> An active participation by all in a collaborative culture means
> that everyone takes responsibility for learning. Teachers and
> others working in such communities will discuss their work
> openly and seek to improve and develop their pedagogy through
> collaborative enquiry and the sharing of good practice.
>
> (Earley 2005: 245)

If you are not working in such a culture, your reaction to the reflection
above may be that some of our deepest needs (thinking back to motivation issues) are incapable of being solved by other people given the context
within which we are working. For example, if something like the following applied: 'I would like help in classroom management but feel that I
can't ask Y because she looks down on me and is jealous of my role as
subject leader' or 'I can't ask T because he is responsible for my year group

and will tell the head anything I say'. Approaches to professional development are affected by the physical and human context as shown by Carol Cardno (2006) in our scenario of development in action. They draw upon relationships with implications for leadership in increasingly diverse communities; communication between people and within the organizational community, and the philosophy underpinning the development of the organization.

This raises questions about the culture and climate of the organization – is it conducive to facilitation in all its forms? The strongest support for teaching and learning occurs where there is a shared vision as identified in Chapter 2. Another important concept is that of respect. Cooney (2006) makes this point in discussing research on a greater level of personalization for pupils so that learning could be tailored to individual needs:

> The main driver for increased personalization was the leaders' set of core values. Just as the children had emphasized friendship as the thing they valued most, the head teachers had built person-centred cultures within their schools based on the premise that each person is worthy of the greatest respect. The school leaders were passionate advocates of placing the child's needs at the heart of all the school did. Creating the climate for positive relationships to flourish was seen as fundamental to the health of the learning community.
>
> (Cooney 2006: 14)

As we approach the end of this chapter on professional and organizational development and its impact, our message is that helping organizations to know what their vision is, to know strategies by which this could be achieved, to enthuse teachers and learners in the task, and to monitor and evaluate the impact of perceived changes requires a culture of joint involvement. Specifically, this can be in a changing series of known tasks cooperatively undertaken, giving equality of opportunity to all, whatever the diversity of the context and participants. This was an emerging finding from Cardno's work set out in the scenario.

But this sort of change can be encouraged on a district-wide as well as a local level. The *Final Evaluation Report of the Manitoba School Improvement Programme,* reporting on work in the period from 1991 to 2003, offers a full account of the way in which change, to enhance school effectiveness as an objective, has been managed in 31 secondary schools (Earl and Lee 2003). Each school developed its own plans and was supported in implementing these by university and district advisory external agencies. The resourcing has allowed for extensive professional development – and, possibly more important, dialogue. This dialogue not only is within the schools but also incorporates governmental and divisional staff so that support can be negotiated to maintain a cycle of continuous improvement through repeated challenges to established practices and beliefs. That is the core of organizational development.

Sustained evaluation and consequent change is dependent upon both internal and external pressures:

> Whether or not innovations are embedded and sustained will depend, not only on the capacity of schools and those connected to them, but also on the infrastructures of pressure and support, and the broader policy and political context in which the schools reside.
>
> (Earl and Lee 1998: 8)

While these conclusions relate to a large number of schools within a school district, they do exemplify the ways in which personal and professional development can be attained. The starting point, as we have seen, has to be an awareness of what is needed if the organization is to meet its stated aims and objectives. The very word awareness can be glibly used – it requires an understanding of where we are and where we are going and interactions and achievements within the teaching arena are fundamental to this. Mentoring, coaching and facilitating offer approaches to influence development and through this can affect attitudes, social justice and institutional outcomes. The sum total of these interactions determines the culture of the organization. So, rather like steering a large ship into port, leadership has to nudge the organization gently towards its objectives.

Summary

This chapter is concerned with the importance and facilitation of learning and development for the individual and the organization. Starting from the notion of the learning community, we then considered the learning of adults and how different individuals have different learning approaches. The scenario gave an example of organizational learning. Learning through observation is particularly important in relation to teaching and learning but can only occur successfully in an open culture. The last section of the chapter focused on the idea of building a learning culture using the three important and related concepts for the learning community of mentoring, coaching and facilitating.

Further reading

It might seem that there is a great deal to do in relation to development of the organization, be it school or college. Development is a complex process and there are so many influences. There is need to think about the skills of leadership within the organization and this is dealt with in very practical ways by the following book: Stone, B. (2004) *The Inner Warrior: Developing the Courage for Personal and Organisational Change.* London: Palgrave-Macmillan.

Looking at teachers as part of a learning community, the following book might have the last word because it stresses the need for communication between all sectors of schools and colleges: Lieberman, A. and Miller, L. (eds) (2008) *Teachers in Professional Communities: Improving Teaching and Learning (Series on School Reform).* New York: Teachers College Press.

Endnote

This book has focused on a number of interrelated skills related to the leadership and management of people in education. The skills themselves are evolving and we have to recognize that the context in which educationalists operate is also evolving.

We commented in the Introduction on the changing understanding of leadership. Perhaps particularly in Western democracies, there is growing approval of forms of distributed leadership with the recognition that leadership is not vested in one individual at the top of a hierarchy. This change, although not necessarily universal, has implications for a more democratic and participatory form of leadership and management in our schools and colleges.

At the same time, there are countervailing tendencies. In many countries including England, there have been changes in educational policy that have introduced a greater level of control and accountability, for example through inspection, and have introduced ideas of the market into education so that schools and colleges are competing for pupils. Ryan and Rottmann (2009: 478) claim that: 'Given the current regulatory context and preoccupation with the market, it will not be easy to introduce, promote or sustain democratic practice in schools.' It may not be easy, but it is still both important and possible.

There is steady change involving gender and leadership. Although there is still a tendency to automatically identify leadership with the male (Schein 2001), more women are emerging in leadership roles in education, although 'there is no doubt from the evidence . . . that being a woman and a head teacher is a very different experience from being a man and a head teacher' (Coleman 2002: 155) and what applies to head teachers will apply just as much in any leadership role. The other change related to gender is that of work–life balance. Holding a leadership role is demanding and time consuming and has implications for family life. At present that applies much more to women than men, because women still tend to take major responsibility for home and children. One outcome is that fewer women are likely to take up leadership roles. However, men also want to play a part in family life and attitudes are slowly changing with regard to domestic stereotypes and the responsibility for child and elder care.

Changes in the wider society have meant that there is much freer movement across national boundaries. Migration for economic and political reasons has changed what were relatively homogenous populations to be a diverse mix of ethnicities and religions.

Throughout the book we have commented on how people are labelled as 'outsiders' and educators need to examine their understanding and develop critical consciousness in relation to diversity, not only in relation to ethnicity, but also in relation to any of the qualities that mark us out as 'different' in some way to the dominant groups in our societies. Each chapter has focused on a different skill but has emphasized the need for reflection in exercising that skill. Stereotypes provide easy short cuts in how we perceive each other. However, we hope that this book will serve to remind you to look through a different 'lens' and see beyond stereotypes to the value of each individual and what they can contribute.

References

Acker, R.V., Boreson, L., Gable, R.A. and Potterton, T. (2005) Are we on the right course? Lessons learned about current FBA/BIP. *Practices in Schools* 14(1): 35–56.

Ackerman, R.J. and Maslin-Ostrowski, P. (2004) The wounded leader and emotional learning in the schoolhouse. *School Leadership and Management* 24(3): 312–328.

Adair, J. (1986) *Effective Teambuilding*. London: Pan.

Adair, J. (1988) *Effective Time Management*. London: Pan.

Allard, R.G. (1988) *Finding Time: Relieving Time Constraints on Senior Staff in Secondary Schools*. Sheffield Papers in Education Management 72. Sheffield: Sheffield City Polytechnic.

Angelique, H., Kyle, K. and Taylor, E. (2002) Mentors and muses: New strategies for academic success. *Innovative Higher Education* 26(3): 195–209.

Arcaro, J. (1995) *Teams in Education: Creating an Integrated Approach*. New York: CRC Press.

Argyris, C. and Schon, D. (1981) *Organizational Learning: A Theory of Action Perspective*. London: Addison-Wesley.

Armstrong, M. (1994) *How To Be an Even Better Manager. London:* Kogan Page.

Armstrong, M. (1999) *A Handbook of Human Resource Management Practice*, 7th edn. London: Kogan Page.

Avolio, B.J. (1999) *Full Leadership Development: Building the Vital Forces in Organizations*. Thousand Oaks, CA: Sage.

Back, K. and Back, K. (1990) *Assertiveness at Work: A Practical Guide to Handling Awkward Situations*. London: McGraw-Hill.

Ball, S.J. (1987) *The Micropolitics of the School*. London: Methuen.

Ball, S.J. (2008) *The Education Debate*. Bristol: Policy Press.

Barrett, M. and Davidson, M.J. (eds) (2006) *Gender and Communication at Work*. Aldershot, Ashgate.

Bassett, S. (2001) The use of phenomenology in management research: An exploration of the learners' experience of coach-mentoring in the workplace. Paper presented at the Qualitative Evidence-Based Practice Conference, Coventry, May.

Baxter, J. (2006) Putting gender in its place: A case study on construction speaker identities in a management meeting, in M. Barrett and

M. Davidson (eds) *Gender and Communication at Work*. Aldershot, Ashgate.

Beare, H., Caldwell, B. and Millikan, R. (1989) *Creating an Excellent School: Some New Management Techniques*. London: Routledge.

Begley, P. (2003) In pursuit of authentic school leadership practices. In P. Begley and O. Johansson (eds) *The Ethical Dimensions of School Leadership*. London: Kluwer.

Begley, P. (2004) Understanding valuation processes: Exploring the linkage between motivation and action. *International Studies in Educational Administration* 32(2): 4–17.

Belbin, R.M. (1993) *Team Roles at Work*. Oxford: Butterworth Heinemann.

Berger, P. and Luckmann, T. (1991) *The Social Construction of Reality*. London: Penguin.

Bhattacharya, G., Ison, L. and Blair, M. (2003) *Minority Ethnic Attainment and Participation Education and Training: The Evidence*. London: DfES.

Blandford, S. and Shaw, M. (eds) (2001) *Managing International Schools*. London: Routledge-Falmer.

Bloom, G., Castagna, C., Moir, E. and Warren, B. (2005) *Blended Coaching: Skills and Strategies to Support Principal Development*. New York: Sage.

Boeree, G. (1999) *Personality Theories Abraham Maslow*. Shippensburg University. Available at www.ship.edu/%7Ecgboeree/perscontents.html (accessed 15 October 2009).

Bottery, M. (2004) *The Challenges of Educational Leadership*. London: Paul Chapman.

Brookfield, S. (1987) *Developing Critical Thinkers*. Milton Keynes: Open University Press.

Brundrett, M. and Anderson de Cuevas, R. (2008) Setting an agenda for the development of the next generation of school leaders: A commitment to social justice or simply making up the numbers? *School Leadership and Management* 28(3): 247–260.

Bubb, S. and Earley, P. (2004) *Managing Teacher Workload: Work-Life Balance and Wellbeing*. London: Paul Chapman.

Buchanan, D. and Huczynski, A. (1997) *Organizational Behaviour: An Introductory Text*, 3rd edn. Harlow: Prentice Hall.

Bush, T. (2003) *Theories of Educational Leadership and Management*, 3rd edn. London: Sage.

Bush, T. and Middlewood, D. (2005) *Leading and Managing People in Education*. London: Paul Chapman.

Bush, T., Cardno, C., Glover, D. and Sood, K. (2004) *First Interim Report on BMEL Leadership*. Nottingham: NCSL.

Bush, T., Glover, D., Sood, K., Cardno, C., Moloi, K., Potgeiter, G. and Tangie, K. (2005) *Black and Minority Ethnic Leaders: Final Report to the*

National College for School Leadership. Lincoln: International Institute for Education Leadership.

Bush, T., Glover, D. and Sood, K. (2006) Black and minority ethnic leaders in England: A portrait. *School Leadership and Management* 26(3): 289–305.

Bush, T., Glover, D. and Middlewood, T. (2008) *First Interim Report on Succession Planning to NCSL.* Unpublished report. Nottingham: NCSL.

Busher, H. (2001) The micro-politics of change: Improvement and effectiveness in schools, in A. Harris and N. Bennett (eds) *School Effectiveness and School Improvement: Alternative Perspectives.* London: Continuum.

Campbell, C., Gold, A. and Lunt, I. (2003) Articulating leadership values in action: Conversations with school leaders. *International Journal of Leadership in Education* 6(3): 203–221.

Canter, L. and Canter, M. (2001) *Assertive Discipline: Positive Behaviour Management for To-day's Classroom,* 3rd edn. New York: Perfect Books.

Capper, C., Theoharis, G. and Sebastian, J. (2006) Toward a framework for preparing leaders for social justice. *Journal of Educational Administration* 44(3): 209–224.

Cardno, C. (1999) Taking the team by the tail: An examination of the potency and demands of team contribution to an organizational learning culture. Paper presented at AARE-NZARE Conference, Melbourne, November.

Cardno, C. (2002) Team learning: Opportunities and challenges for school leaders. *School Leadership and Management* 22(2): 211–223.

Cardno, C. (2006) Leading change from within: Action research to strengthen curriculum leadership in a primary school. *School Leadership and Management* 26(5): 453–471.

Carli, L.L. (2006) Gender and workplace issues, in M. Barrett and M. Davidson (eds) *Gender and Communication in the Workplace.* Aldershot, Ashgate.

Carroll, G.R. and Hannan, M.T. (2000) Why corporate demography matters: Policy implications of organizational diversity. *California Management Review* 42(3): 148–163.

Carroll, D. (2005) Learning through interactive talk: A school-based mentor teacher study group as a context for professional learning. *Teaching and Teacher Education* 21(5): 457–473.

Caspi, A., Elder, G.H. and Bern, D. (1987) Moving against the world: Life course patterns of explosive children. *Developmental Psychology* 23(2): 308–313.

Caspi, A., Elder, G.H. and Bern, D. (1988) Moving against the world: Life course patterns of shy children. *Developmental Psychology* 24(6): 824–831.

Chen, Guoquan, Liu, Chunhong and Tjosvold, D. (2005) Conflict management for effective top management teams and innovation in China. *Journal of Management Studies* 42(2): 278–300.

Chugh, D. and Brief, A.P. (2008) Introduction: Where the sweet spot is. Studying diversity in organizations, in A.P. Brief (ed.) *Diversity at Work*. Cambridge: Cambridge University Press.

Coleman, M. (2002) *Women as Headteachers: Striking the Balance*. Stoke-on-Trent: Trentham.

Coleman, M. (2005) *Gender and Headship in the Twenty-first Century*. Nottingham: NCSL. An executive summary is available at www.nationalcollege.org.uk/gender-and-headship-in-the-21st-century-summary.pdf (accessed 26 October 2009).

Coleman, M. (2007) Gender and educational leadership in England: A comparison of secondary headteachers' views over time. *School Leadership and Management* 27(4): 383–399.

Coleman, M. (2009a) *Women Only Networks: Four Case Studies*. London: WLE Centre, Institute of Education.

Coleman, M. (2009b) Senior women in secondary schools: A case study. Unpublished paper. London: WLE Centre, Institute of Education.

Coleman, M. and Campbell Stephens, R. (2009) *Factors Affecting Career Progress: The Perceptions of Black and Minority Ethnic (BME) Deputy and Assistant Head Teachers who had Participated in the Programme 'Investing in Diversity'*. Occasional Papers in Work-based Learning. London: WLE Centre, Institute of Education.

Coleman, M. and Campbell Stephens, R. (2010) Perceptions of career progress: The experience of BME school leaders. *School Leadership and Management*, 30(1): 35–50.

Coleman, M., Qiang, H. and Li, Y. (1998) Women in educational management in China: Experience in Shaanxi Province. *Compare* 28(2): 141–154.

Cooney, K. (2006) *'Are you learnin' us to-day, Miss?' Developing Learning for Assessment as Personalised Practice*. Nottingham: NCSL.

Covey, S. (1989) *The 7 Habits of Highly Effective People: Powerful Lessons in Personal Change*. New York: Simon & Schuster.

Crawford, M. (1997) Managing stress in education, in T. Bush and D. Middlewood (eds) *Managing People in Education*. London: Paul Chapman.

Crawford, M. (2009) *Getting to the Heart of Leadership: Emotion and the Educational Leader*. London: Sage.

Creasy, J. and Patterson, F. (2005) *Leading Personalised Learning*. Nottingham: NCSL.

Cutler, T. and Waine, B. (2001) Report: Performance management – The key to higher standards in schools? *Public Money & Management* 21(2): 69–72.

Davidson, M.J. (1997) *The Black and Ethnic Minority Woman Manager: Cracking the Concrete Ceiling.* London: Paul Chapman.

Deal, T. (1985) The symbolism of effective schools. *Elementary School Journal* 85(5): 601–620.

Deal, T. and Peterson, K. (1999) *Shaping School Culture: The Heart of Leadership.* San Francisco, CA: Jossey-Bass.

Deem, R. and Morley, L. (2006) Diversity in the academy? Staff perceptions of equality policies in six contemporary higher education institutions. *Policy Futures in Education* 4(2): 185–202.

Department for Children, Schools and Families (DCSF) (2008) *School Workforce in England January 2008.* London: DCSF.

Department for Education and Employment (DfEE) (2000) *Performance Management Framework.* London: DfEE.

Department for Education and Skills (DfES) (2006) *Ethnicity and Education: The Evidence on Minority Ethnic Pupils Aged 5–16.* London: DfES.

Earl, L. and Lee, L. (1998) *Evaluation of the Manitoba School Improvement Program.* Winnipeg: Manitoba School Improvement Program.

Earl, L. and Lee, L. (2003) *Final Evaluation Report of the Manitoba School Improvement Program.* Winnipeg: Manitoba School Improvement Program.

Earley, P. (2005) Continuing professional development: The learning community, in M. Coleman and P. Earley, *Leadership and Management in Education: Cultures, Change and Context.* Oxford: Oxford University Press.

Ely, R.J. and Morgan Roberts, L. (2008) Shifting frames in team-diversity research: From difference to relationships, in A.P. Brief (ed.) *Diversity at Work.* Cambridge: Cambridge University Press.

Equality and Human Rights Commission (2008) *Sex and Power 2008.* Available at www.equalityhumanrights.com/uploaded_files/sex_and_power_2008_pdf.pdf (accessed 26 October 2009).

Evans, L. (2003) Leadership role: Morale, job-satisfaction and motivation, in L. Kydd, L. Anderson and W. Newton (eds) *Leading People and Teams in Education.* London: Paul Chapman.

Everard, K.B., Morris, G. and Wilson, I. (2004) Managing meetings, in *Effective School Management,* 4th edn, London: Paul Chapman.

Fineman, S. (2000) Commodifying the emotionally intelligent, in S. Fineman (ed.) *Emotion in Organizations.* London: Sage.

Fineman, S. (2003) *Understanding Emotion at Work.* London: Sage.

Fisher, R. and Ury, W. (1981) *Getting to Yes.* London: Arrow.

Fiske, S.T. and Lee, T.L. (2008) Stereotypes and prejudice create workplace discrimination, in A.P. Brief (ed.) *Diversity at Work.* Cambridge: Cambridge University Press.

Fitzgerald, T., Youngs, H. and Grootenboer, P. (2003) Bureaucratic control or professional autonomy? Performance management in New Zealand schools. *School Leadership and Management* 23(1): 91–105.

Fletcher, J.K. and Kaeufer, K. (2003) Shared leadership: Paradox and possibility, in C. Pearce and J. Conger (eds) *Shared Leadership: Current Thinking, Future Trends*. Thousand Oaks, CA: Sage.

Foskett, N. and Hemsley-Brown, J. (1999) Communicating the organisation, in J. Lumby and N. Foskett (eds) *Managing External Relations in Schools and Colleges*. London: Paul Chapman.

Freire, P. (1970) Pedagogy of the Oppressed, in D.J. Flinders and S.J. Thornton (eds) *Curriculum Studies Reader*. New York: Routledge.

Fuller, K. (2009) Women secondary head teachers: Alive and well in Birmingham at the beginning of the twenty-first century. *Management in Education* 23(1): 19–31.

Galton, M. and MacBeath, J. (2008) *Teachers under Pressure*. Co-publication with the National Union of Teachers (NUT). London: Paul Chapman.

Gardner, H. (1983) *Frames of Mind: The Theory of Multiple Intelligences*. New York: Basic Books.

Gillborn, D. (2008) Coincidence or conspiracy? Whiteness, policy and the persistence of the Black/White achievement gap. *Educational Review* 60(3): 229–248.

Glover, D. (2006) Contribution, in T. Bush, D. Glover and K. Sood, Black and minority ethnic leaders in England: A portrait. *School Leadership and Management* 26(3): 289–305.

Glover, D., Miller, D.J., Averis, D. and Door, V. (2007) The evolution of an effective pedagogy for teachers using the interactive whiteboard in mathematics and modern languages: An empirical analysis from the secondary sector. *Learning, Media and Technology* 32(1): 5–20.

Gold, A. (1998) *Head of Department: Principles in Practice*. London: Cassell.

Gold, A. (2004) *Values and Leadership*. London: Institute of Education, University of London.

Gold, A. and Evans, J. (1998) *Reflecting on School Management*. London: Falmer.

Gold, A., Evans, J., Earley, P., Halpin, D. and Collarbone, P. (2003) Principled principals? Values driven leadership: Evidence from ten case studies of 'outstanding' school leaders. *Educational Administration, Management and Leadership* 31(2): 127–138.

Goleman, D. (1995) *Emotional Intelligence: What It Is and Why It Can Matter More than IQ*. New York: Bantam.

Goleman, D. (1998) *Working with Emotional Intelligence*. London: Bloomsbury.

Gosetti, P. and Rusch, E. (1995) Reexamining educational leadership: Challenging assumptions, in D.M. Dunlap and P.A. Schmuck (eds) *Women Leading in Education*. Albany, NY: State University of New York.

Graham, J.L. (1987) A theory of interorganizational negotiations. *Research in Marketing* 9: 163–183.

Graham-Jolly, M. and Peacock, M. (2000) More than one lesson: The Thousand Schools Project in KwaZulu-Natal, South Africa. *International Journal of Educational Development* 20(5): 397–405.

Grant, C. (2006) Teacher leadership emerging voices on teacher leadership: Some South African views. *Educational Management Administration and Leadership* 34(4): 511–532.

Gratton, L., Keland, E., Voigt, A., Walker, L. and Wolfram, H-J. (2007) *Innovative Potential: Men and Women in Teams*. London: Lehman Brothers Centre for Women in Business, London Business School.

Gross, J.J. and John, O.P. (2002) Wise emotion regulation, in L. Feldman Barrett and P. Salovey (eds) *The Wisdom of Feeling*. New York: Guilford.

Halai, A. (2006) Mentoring in-service teachers: Issues of role diversity. *Teaching and Teacher Education* 22(6): 700–710.

Hammersley-Fletcher, L. and Adnett, N. (2009) Empowerment or prescription? Workforce remodelling at the national and school level. *Educational Management, Administration and Leadership* 37(2): 180–198.

Handy, C.B. (1993) *Understanding Organizations*, 4th edn. Harmondsworth: Penguin.

Handy, C.B. and Aitken, R. (1986) *Understanding Schools as Organizations*. Harmondsworth: Penguin.

Harber, C. and Davies, L. (1997) *School Management and Effectiveness in Developing Countries*. London: Cassell.

Hargie, C., Toursin, D. and Hargie, O. (1994) Managers communicating. *International Journal of Educational Management* 8(6): 23–28.

Hargreaves, A. (2004) Inclusive and exclusive educational change: Emotional responses of teachers and implications for leadership. *School Leadership and Management* 24(2): 287–309.

Hargreaves, E. (2005) Assessment for learning? Thinking outside the (black) box. *Cambridge Journal of Education* 35(2): 213–224.

Harris, A. and Goodall, J. (2008) Do parents know they matter? Engaging all parents in learning. *Educational Research* 50(3): 277–289.

Harris, A., Muijs, D. and Crawford, M. (2003) *Deputy and Assistant Heads: Building Leadership Potential*. Nottingham: NCSL.

Haviland-Jones, J. and Kahlbaugh, P. (2004) Emotion and identity, in M. Lewis and J. Haviland-Jones (eds) *Handbook of Emotions*. New York: Guilford.

Hay McBer (2000) *A Model of Teacher Effectiveness*. London: Department for Education and Employment.

Haydon, G. (2007) *Values for Educational Leadership*. London: Sage.

Hayes, D. (1996) Introduction of collaborative decision-making in a primary school. *Educational Management and Administration* 24(3): 291–299.

Health and Safety Commission (HSC, Education Service Advisory Committee) (1990) *Managing Occupational Stress: A Guide for Managers and Teachers in the Schools Sector*. London: HMSO.

Hean, D.S. and Garrett, R. (2001) Sources of job satisfaction in secondary science school teachers in Chile. *Compare* 31(3): 363–379.

Herzberg, F. (1966) The motivation-hygiene theory, in D. Pugh (ed.) *Organization Theory: Selected Readings*. Harmondsworth: Penguin.

Hochschild, A.R. (1983) *The Managed Heart: Commercialization of Human Feeling*. Berkeley, CA: University of California Press.

Hodgkinson, C. (1991) *Educational Leadership: The Moral Art*. Albany, NY: State University of New York Press.

Hofstede, G. (1991) *Cultures and Organization*. London: HarperCollins.

Honey, P. (2009) *Learning Styles Questionnaire*. Maidenhead: Peter Honey Publications.

Honey, P. and Mumford, A. (1988) *Manual of Learning Styles*. Maidenhead: Peter Honey Publications.

Hoy, W.K. and Miskel, C.G. (2005) *Educational Administration: Theory, Research, and Practice*, 7th edn. Boston, MA: McGraw-Hill International.

Hoyle, E. (1986) *Politics of School Management*. Sevenoaks: Hodder & Stoughton.

Ian Dodds Consulting (2006) *Taking an Honest Look at your Business Culture from a Diversity Perspective*. Available at www.iandoddsconsulting.com/features.html (accessed 31 August 2006).

Jackson, S.E., Joshi, A. and Erhardt, N.L. (2003) Recent research on team and organizational diversity: SWOT analysis and implications. *Journal of Management* 29(6): 801–830.

Jehn, K.A., Greer, L.L. and Rupert, J. (2008) Diversity, conflict, and their consequences, in A.P. Brief (ed.) *Diversity at Work*. Cambridge: Cambridge University Press.

Jennings, K. and Lomas, L. (2003) Implementing performance management for headteachers in English secondary schools. *Educational Management Administration and Leadership* 31(4): 369–383.

Johnson, P.H., Daly, P., Chrispeels, A.J. and Burke, J.H. (2008) Aligning mental models of district and school leadership teams for reform coherence. *Education and Urban Society* 40(6): 730–750.

Jones, J. (2005) *Management Skills in Schools: A Resource for School Leaders*. London: Paul Chapman.

Kanter, R. (1983) *The Change Masters*. London: Unwin Hyman.

Kaplan, R.S. and Norton, D.P. (1996) *The Balanced Scorecard*. Boston, MA: Harvard Business School.

Kasoulides, Y. and Pashiardis, P. (2004) The bad news: time flies ... The good news: the joystick is in your hands! A case study concerning the way a principal manages his time. Paper presented at CCEAM conference, Hong Kong, October.

Kelly, A. (2002) *Team Talk: Sharing Leadership in Primary Schools*. Summary Practitioner Enquiry Report. Nottingham: NCSL.

Kennedy, G. (1989) *Everything is Negotiable:* London: Arrow.

Kolb, D. (1984) *Experiential Learning: Experience as a Source of Learning and Development*. Englewood Cliffs, NJ: Prentice Hall.

Kramer, V.W., Konrad, A.M. and Erkut, S. (2006) *Critical Mass on Corporate Boards: Why Three or More Women Enhance Governance. Executive Summary*. Wellesley, MA: Wellesley Centers for Women's Publication Office.

Kulik, C.T. and Roberson, L. (2008) Diversity initiative effectiveness: What organizations can (and cannot) expect from diversity recruitment, diversity training and formal mentoring programs, in A.P. Brief (ed.) *Diversity at Work*. Cambridge: Cambridge University Press.

Kwok Sai Wong and Wai Hing Cheuk (2005) Job-related stress and social support in kindergarten principals: The case of Macau. *International Journal of Educational Management* 19(3): 183–196.

Langlois, L. (2004) Responding ethically: Complex decision-making by school district superintendents. *International Studies in Educational Administration* 32(2): 78–93.

Lárusdóttir, S.H. (2008) Leadership, values and gender: A study of Icelandic headteachers. Unpublished PhD thesis, University of London.

Law, S. and Glover, D. (2000) *Educational Leadership and Learning: Practice, Policy and Research*. Buckingham: Open University Press.

Lazarus, R.S. (1991) *Emotion and Adaptation*. Oxford: Oxford University Press.

Leithwood, K. with Jantzi, D. and Steinbach, R. (1999) *Changing Leadership for Changing Times*. Maidenhead: Open University Press.

Leithwood, K., Mascall, B. and Strauss, T. (eds) (2009) *Distributed Leadership According to the Evidence*. New York: Routledge.

Leonard, D. (2001) *A Woman's Guide to Doctoral Studies*. Buckingham: Open University Press.

Lowe, T.J. and Pollard, I.W (1989) Negotiation skills, in C. Riches and G. Morgan (eds) *Human Resource Management in Education*. Buckingham: Open University Press.

Luck, C. (2003) *It's Good to Talk*. Nottingham: NCSL.

Lugg, C. and Tooms, A. (2010) A shadow of ourselves: Identity erasure and the politics of queer leadership. *School Leadership and Management,* 30(1): 77–90.

Lumby, J. with Coleman, M. (2008) *Leadership and Diversity: Challenging Theory and Practice in Education.* London: Sage.

Lupton, D. (1998) *The Emotional Self: A Socio-cultural Exploration.* London: Sage.

McGregor, D. (1960) *The Human Side of Enterprise.* New York: McGraw-Hill.

Mackay, F. and Etienne, J. (2006) Black managers in further education: Career hopes and hesitations. *Educational Management, Administration and Leadership* 34(1): 9–28.

McKenley, J. and Gordon, G. (2002) *Challenge Plus: The Experience of Black and Minority Ethnic School Leaders.* Nottingham: NCSL.

Mackeracher, D. (2004) *Making Sense of Adult Learning.* Toronto: University of Toronto Press.

Maslow, A. (1943) A theory of human motivation. *Psychological Review* 1: 370–396.

Mathews, P. (2003) Academic mentoring: Enhancing the use of scarce resources. *Educational Management Administration and Leadership* 31(3): 313.

Mikatavage, R., Aldrich, J. and Ford, M. (2002) Immigration, ethnic cultures and achievement: Working with communities, parents and teachers. *MultiCultural Review* 11(3): 38–41.

Moll, L.C. (1995) The cultural mediation of educational practice. Invited paper, The Dean's Forum, College of Education, University of Arizona, December.

Morgan, C., Hall, V. and Mackay, H. (1983) *The Selection of Secondary Headteachers.* Milton Keynes: Open University Press.

Morrison, K. (1998) *Management Theories for Educational Change.* London: Paul Chapman.

Morriss, S.B., Coleman, M. and Low Guat Tin (1999) Leadership stereotypes and female Singaporean principals. *Compare* 29(2): 191–202.

Moss, G. (1999) Drawing on personal resources. *Managing Schools To-day* 8(5): 27–28.

Moss, J. (2008) Leading professional learning in an Australian secondary school through school-university partnerships. *Asia Pacific Journal of Teacher Education* 36(4): 345–357.

Muijs, D. and Harris, A. (2003) Teacher leadership – Improvement through empowerment? An overview of the literature. *Educational Management Administration and Leadership* 31(4): 437–448.

Mulholland, G. (1991) *The Language of Negotiation.* London: Cassell.

Mullins, L. (1993) *Management and Organisational Behaviour.* London: Pitman.

National Assembly of Wales (2005) *Revised National Standards for Head-teachers in Wales*. Cardiff: Welsh Assembly.

Nias, J., Southworth, G. and Yeomans, R. (1989) *Staff Relationships in the Primary School*. London: Cassell.

North West Change Centre of Manchester Business School (2002) *Diversity – The Key to Modernization and the Bedrock of Democracy*. Manchester: Manchester Business School.

Nussbaum, M. (1999) *Women and Human Development: The Capabilities Approach*. Cambridge: Cambridge: University Press.

Ofsted (2004) *Remodelling the School Workforce*. Document HMI 2298. London: HMSO.

Ogawa, R.T. and Bossert, S.T. (1997) Leadership as an organisational quality, in M. Crawford, L. Kydd and C. Riches (eds) *Leadership and Teams in Educational Management*. Buckingham: Open University Press.

O'Neill, J. (2003) Managing through teams, in L. Kydd, L. Anderson and W. Newton (eds) *Leading People and Teams in Education*. London: Paul Chapman.

Ostell, A. and Oakland, S. (1995) *Headteacher Stress, Coping and Health*. Aldershot: Avebury.

O'Sullivan, F., Jones, K. and Reid, K.J. (1997) The development of staff, in L. Kydd, K. Crawford and C. Riches (eds) *Professional Development for Educational Management*. Buckingham: Open University Press.

O'Sullivan, M. (2006) Lesson observation and quality in primary education as contextual teaching and learning processes. *International Journal of Educational Development* 26: 246–260.

Powney, J., Wilson, V. and Hall, S. (2003) *Teachers Careers: The Impact of Age, Disability, Ethnicity, Gender and Sexual Orientation*. London: DfES.

PricewaterhouseCooper (2001) *Teacher Workload Study: Interim Report*. London: DfES.

PricewaterhouseCooper (2007) *Independent Study into School Leadership*. London: DfES.

Prosser, J. (1999) *School Culture*. London: Paul Chapman.

Ragins, B.R. (2002) Understanding diversified mentoring relationships: Challenges in diversified mentoring programmes, in D. Clutterbuck and B.R. Ragins (eds) *Mentoring and Diversity*. Oxford: Butterworth Heinemann.

Rasberry, P.W. and Lemoine, L. (1986) *Effective Managerial Communication*. Boston, MA: Kent.

Reynolds, D. (2007) *Schools Learning from their Best: The Within School Variation Project*. Nottingham: NCSL.

Riches, C. (1997) Communication and educational management, in M. Crawford, L. Kyyd and C. Riches (eds) *Leadership and Teams in Educational Management*. Buckingham: Open University Press.

Rigg, C. and Richards, C. (eds) (2005) *Action Learning, Leadership and Organisational Development in Public Services*. London: Routledge.

Robbins, S. and Trabichet, L. (2009) Ethical decision-making by educational leaders: Its foundations, culture and more recent perspectives. *Management in Education* 23(2): 51–56.

Roberts, J. (undated [c.1995]) *Didn't I just say that? The Gender Dynamics of Decision Making*. Research paper 1. Canberra: Australian Government Publishing Service.

Robertson, C., Robins, A. and Cox, R. (2009) Co-constructing an academic community ethos – Challenging culture and managing change in higher education: A case study undertaken over two years. *Management in Education* 23(1): 32–40.

Russell, J. (2009) Women can't depend on liberals for equality: We need radical action now. *Guardian*, 11 May.

Ryan, J. (2006) *Inclusive Leadership*. San Francisco, CA: Jossey-Bass.

Ryan, J. and Rottmann, C. (2009) Struggling for democracy: Administrative communication in a diverse school context, *Educational Management Administration and Leadership* 37(4): 473–496.

Saarni, C. (2000) The social context of emotional development, in M. Lewis and J. Haviland-Jones (eds) *Handbook of Emotions*. New York: Guilford.

Salo, P. (2008) Decision-making as a struggle and a play. *Educational Management, Administration and Leadership* 36(4): 495–510.

Salovey, P. and Mayer, P. (1990) Emotional intelligence. *Imagination, Cognition and Personality* 9(3): 185–211.

Salovey, P. and Mayer, P. (2001) Emotional intelligence, in K. Oatley and J.M. Jenkins (eds) *Human Emotion: A Reader*. Oxford: Blackwell.

Salovey, P., Bedwell, B., Detweiler, J. and Mayer, J. (2000) Current directions in emotional intelligence research, in M. Lewis and J. Haviland-Jones (eds) *Handbook of Emotions*. New York: Guilford.

Santoro, N. (2009) Teaching in culturally diverse contexts: What knowledge about 'self' and 'others' do teachers need? *Journal of Education for Teaching* 35(1): 33–45.

Schacter, S. (1951) Deviation, rejection and communication, in D. Cartwright and A. Zander (eds) *Group Dynamics*. London: Tavistock.

Schein, V.E. (2001) A global look at psychological barriers to women's progress in management. *Journal of Social Issues* 67: 675–688.

Schick-Case, S. (1994) Gender differences in communication and behaviour in organizations, in M.J. Davidson and R.J. Burke *Women in Management: Current Research Issues*. London: Paul Chapman.

Sen, R.S. and Samdup, P.E. (2009) Revisiting gender in open and distance learning: An independent variable or a mediated reality? *Open Learning* 24(2): 165–185.

Shah, S. (2008) Leading multi-ethnic schools: Adjustments in concepts and practices for engaging with diversity. *British Journal of Sociology of Education* 29(5): 523–536.

Shah, S. and Shaikh, J. (2010) Leadership progression of Muslim male teachers: Interplay of ethnicity, faith and visibility. *School Leadership and Management,* 30(1): 19–34.

Shaw, M. (2001) Managing mixed-culture teams in international schools, in S. Blandford and M. Shaw (eds) *Managing International Schools.* London: Routledge.

Sinclair, A. (1999) *Doing Management Differently.* Melbourne: Melbourne University Press.

Solomon, R.C. (2000) The philosophy of emotions, in M. Lewis and J. Haviland Jones (eds) *Handbook of Emotions.* New York: Guilford.

Southern African Historical Society (Unisa Online) (2006) www.sahs.org.za (accessed 26 October 2009).

Staessens. K. and Vandenberghe, R. (1994) Vision as a core component in school culture. *Journal of Curriculum Studies* 26(2): 187–200.

Stead, V. (2006) Mentoring: A model for leadership development? *International Journal of Training and Development* 9(3): 170–182.

Stone, D. and Colella, A. (1996) A model of factors affecting the treatment of disabled individuals in organizations. *Academy of Management Review* 12(2): 352–401.

Storey, A. (2002) Performance management in schools: Could the Balanced Scorecard help? *School Leadership and Management* 22(3): 321–338.

Tannenbaum, R. and Schmidt, W.H. (1973) How to choose a leadership pattern. *Harvard Business Review* May–June: 162–180.

Taylor, I. (2007) Pursued by excellence: Rewards and the performance culture in higher education. *Social Work Education* 26(5): 504–519.

Thomas, D. (2008) *Cross-cultural Management: Essential Concepts*, 2nd edn. Thousand Oaks, CA: Sage.

Thomson, R. (2006) Gender and electronic discourse in the workplace, in M. Barrett and M.J. Davidson (eds) *Gender and Communication at Work.* Aldershot: Ashgate.

Travers, C. and Cooper, C. (1996) *Time Management for Teachers.* London: Routledge.

Troman, G. (2003) Teacher stress in the low-trust society, in L. Kydd, L. Anderson and W. Newton (eds) *Leading People and Teams in Education.* London: Paul Chapman.

Trompenaars, F. and Hampden-Turner, C. (1997) *Riding the Waves of Culture.* London: Nicholas Brealey.

Tuckman, B.W. (1965) Developmental sequence in small groups. *Psychological Bulletin* 63(6): 384–399.

Tuckman, B.W. and Jensen, M.A.C. (1977) Stages of small-group development revisited. *Group and Organization Management* 2(4): 419–427.

Tusting, K. and Barton, D. (2006) *Models of Adult Learning: A Literature Review*. London: National Institute of Adult Continuing Education.

Walker, A., Dimmock, C., Stevenson, H., Bignold, B., Shah, S. and Middlewood, D. (2005) *Effective Leadership in Multi-ethnic School*. Nottingham: NCSL.

West, M. (1999) Micropolitics, leadership and all that … The need to increase micropoltical awareness and skills of school leaders. *School Leadership and Management* 19(2): 189–207.

Whitaker, P. (1997) *Primary Schools and the Future*. Buckingham: Open University Press.

Wildy, H., Forster, P., Louden, W. and Wallace, J. (2004) The international study of leadership in education: Monitoring decision making by school leaders. *Journal of Educational Administration* 42(4): 416–430.

Wilkinson, C. (1992) The management of time, in N. Bennett, M. Crawford and C. Riches (eds) *Managing Change in Education: Individual and Organizational Perspectives*. London: Paul Chapman.

Williams, A.P.O. (2009) Leadership at the top: Some insights from a longitudinal case study of a UK business school. *Educational Management Administration and Leadership* 37(1): 127–145.

Williams, G.L. (1994) Observing and recording meetings, in N. Bennett, R. Glatter and R. Levacic (eds) *Improving Educational Management*. London: Paul Chapman.

Woodcock, M. (1985) *Team Development Manual*. Aldershot: Gower.

Woods, P.A. (2005) *Democratic Leadership in Education*. London: Sage and Paul Chapman.

Wright, N. (2003) Principled 'Bastard' Leadership? A rejoinder to Gold, Evans, Earley, Halpin and Collarbone. *Educational Management and Administration* 31(2): 139–143.

Author index

Subject index

WHAT'S WORTH FIGHTING FOR IN HEADSHIP? 2/E

Michael Fullan

In the exciting new edition of this bestselling book, Michael Fullan looks at how much has changed in the world of headship and school improvement in recent decades, and offers key guidelines for being a successful head teacher in the 21st century.

Policymakers and school reformers have increasingly pointed to the head-teacher as the most important agent for change in our schools. The first edition argued that there was little point waiting for the system to improve, and urged headteachers to take charge and to assume that on any given day the system may not know what it is doing. Since then the situation has become even more complex.

The good news is that finally the role of head teacher is being recognized by politicians and policymakers as key, but the bad news is that they are overloaded with initiatives and expectations that serve only to fetter deep action. The irony is that as the head teacher is elevated as critical to success, the headship is sinking - overloaded and pulled down at the same time.

In this completely rewritten and updated new edition, Fullan furnishes six action guidelines for heads, and six for systems to enable them to make dramatic improvements in schools. He seeks a way out of the current dilemma, helping incumbent and would-be head teachers in leveraging action that will positively change the system in both small and large ways.

Contents: *The Overloaded School Head - Leading Legacies - Leading Know-ledgeably - Leading Learning Communities - Leading Systems - Leading WWFF into Action*

2008   80pp

978-0-335-23538-4 (Paperback)

SYSTEM LEADERSHIP IN PRACTICE

Rob Higham; David Hopkins; Peter Matthews

"With all the current interest in system reform and the spread of leadership, System Leadership in Practice is the only book in existence that treats the topic thoroughly and with insight. The authors have written a gem - a book that presents clear conceptual clarity linked to case after case example. They answer the burning question, how can we establish multi-faceted leadership that produces deep and sustained effectiveness."
Michael Fullan, Professor Emeritus of the Ontario Institute for Studies in Education at the University of Toronto

System leadership is a new, exciting and growing phenomenon in education. It refers to leadership that goes beyond a single school, where leaders work directly for the success and welfare of students in other institutions as well as their own.

In this inspirational book, the authors offer you new perspectives, support and guidance – whether you are a school leader, policy-maker or advisor – and show how working collaboratively and leading networks can bring about positive change. They encourage you to innovate, develop rigorous partnerships, take managed risks and deploy resources creatively in order to build sustained improvements in student learning and well-being.

This much-needed book provides the first in-depth analysis of a term on the lips of many in the educational world. There is detailed reference to real cases of system leadership in practice, as well as recent legislation and relevant literature. At a time when prescription, bureaucracy and targets remain for many an impediment to the aims of education, school-led system leadership is seen to offer a means for professionals to take more control of educational renewal.

Contents: *Acknowledgements - Preface - Power to the professionals; the emergence of system leadership - Mapping the system leadership landscape - Leadership of sustained improvement in challenging contexts - Leading innovation and improvement partnerships: the case of leading edge - Leadership in the context of 'Every Child Matters': extended, full service and community schools - Executive leadership and federations - Change agents of school transformation: consultant leaders, national leaders of education and their schools - The prospects for system leadership*

2009   184pp

978-0-335-23611-4 (Paperback)   978-0-335-23612-1 (Hardback)

EVERY SCHOOL A GREAT SCHOOL

David Hopkins

'Every school a great school' is not just a slogan, but an aspiration for the next stage of education reform, in which each student has the opportunity to reach their full potential.

The book argues that, for 'every school a great school' to become a reality, requires a move from individual school improvement efforts and short term objectives to a sustainable system-wide response that seeks to re-establish a balance between national prescription and schools leading reform.

Achieving this goal requires strategies that not only continue to raise standards, but also build capacity within the system. David Hopkins identifies four key educational 'drivers' that, if pursued, have the potential to deliver 'every school a great school':

- Personalized learning
- Professionalized teaching
- Networking and innovation
- Intelligent accountability

The author believes that it is the responsibility of system leaders to mould the four drivers to fit individual school contexts. It is this leadership that enables systemic reform to be generic in terms of overall strategy and specific in adapting to individual and particular situations.

Every School a Great School is inspirational reading for head teachers, senior leaders and managers, researchers, lecturers and those with a passionate interest in improving education for all.

Contents: *Introduction - The Context of System Reform - Every school a great school - From large-scale change to system-wide reform - The Four Drivers of System Reform - Personalized learning - Professionalized teaching - Intelligent accountability - Networking and innovation - Realizing the System Leadership Dividend - The power of system leadership - Moving system leadership to scale - Bibliography - Index*

2007   216pp

978-0-335-22099-1 (Paperback)